Echoes in Mallorca

"Life in the Balearic Islands"

Wesley Baker

First published in 2026
Scott Calvin Publishing
wesleybaker.com

Cover design by germancreative
Front cover image in window © iStock & Shutterstock
Image photographer @ Balate.Dorin

Disclaimer

This book is a memoir based on real events, experiences, and people. While it is rooted in truth, names of individuals and some businesses, including accommodations and specific locations, have been changed to protect privacy and respect confidentiality.

Certain characters are composites or fictionalised to better reflect the emotional truth of events and to maintain narrative clarity. Dialogue has been recreated from memory and is intended to capture the spirit of conversations rather than serve as direct transcripts.

The views expressed are those of the author, as remembered and interpreted at the time of writing. Any resemblance to actual persons, living or dead, or actual events beyond those intended is purely coincidental.

*To all those whose paths we have crossed on my travels
I thank you for your experiences, friendship and the
storytelling along the way, be it on a plane, train, or coach,
or maybe in a hotel, bar, on the beach or in a cafe.*

---

*To my family, your love, and your faith
in me continues to inspire every page I write.*

---

*To all my friends, I value you all and thank you
for being part of my life.*

Prologue

This is the fourth book in the Echoes Travel Memoir series, yet in many ways it is the first.

Before Costa Brava.
Before Andalusia.
Before seasons, friendships, heartbreaks, and the quiet understanding of what it truly meant to live overseas.

This was my beginning, my first taste of life and work beyond the familiar shores of home. The moment when the idea of elsewhere became real.

The Balearic Islands sit in the Mediterranean, off the coast of Spain: Mallorca, Menorca, Ibiza, and Formentera. Over the centuries, they have been places of movement and exchange, shaped by history, culture, and the sea itself. Today, they are among the most loved summer destinations in Europe, known for their beaches, heat, and long, generous days.

But for me, they were something far more personal.

Mallorca, in particular, felt magical from the moment I arrived. An island of contrasts, rugged and mountainous in the north, softer and flatter in the south, with the sea constantly present, lapping gently against its shores. For a young man from Whitstable, in England, it felt like stepping into a dream I hadn't yet dared to imagine.

Here were quiet villages and small towns where time seemed to slow, sitting alongside large tourist resorts alive with laughter, music, and nightlife that spilt effortlessly into the early hours.

It was an island that held both calm and chaos, solitude and connection, often all within the same day.

My time in Mallorca, or as some say Majorca, was a testing ground. A beginning. The place where something shifted quietly inside me.

I didn't know it then, but this island would light the fuse for a lifelong love affair with travel, with living abroad, and with a way of life that would shape everything that followed.

This is where it all began.

It was this wonderful island that quietly stole my soul, and no matter where life has taken me since, it has always held a close and permanent place in my heart. Mallorca was where I tasted independence for the first time: my first cocktails, my first truly lively nights, and my earliest lessons in how to become an overseas travel representative for one of the world's largest travel companies.

But more than that, it was here that I began to grow up.

In the months that followed, the island shaped me in ways I couldn't yet see, through people, places, small mistakes, and moments of unexpected clarity. In the pages that follow, you'll meet a slightly different version of me from the one you may know in the later Echoes books. Less certain. More open. Still finding his feet.

And that is what makes this story special. Not every book and memoir is the same, and that is the beauty of writing them; each is a different part of my story, which I am sharing with you in the hope that it will light a flame of adventure in you or bring back travel memories from another time.

Chapter One

As I sat looking out of the aircraft window, the aqua and deep blues of the Mediterranean Sea below felt both inspiring and quietly magical. Far beneath us, a few large ships moved steadily across the water, their slow progress setting my imagination loose.

In those few suspended minutes, my thoughts drifted back to my grandfather crossing oceans in troop ships during the Second World War, and further still, to the countless centuries of conquest, migration, and trade that had passed across these same waters.

Then the pilot's voice broke through my thoughts.

We were beginning our final approach into Palma de Mallorca. The temperature on the island was a balmy nineteen degrees and sunny, a far cry from the grey, miserable ten degrees I had left behind at London Gatwick only hours earlier.

I leaned closer to the window and caught my first true glimpse of Mallorca. My heart began to pound. Below me rose tall hills that felt more like mountains, their green slopes rolling away toward the sea. As the aircraft banked gently alongside them, I shifted in my seat and peered between the rows ahead, catching a clear view through the open cockpit door as the pilots eased us into our descent.

It was the 1980s, a different time altogether, when the idea of hijacking felt distant, and cockpit doors were often left open. From my seat, I could see the quiet focus of the pilots, hands steady on the controls, guiding us toward an island I didn't yet know would change everything.

On final approach, I could see windmills scattered across the landscape as far as the eye could see, small, white, and beautiful. A surge of excitement rushed through me like never before. I was about to explore something entirely new, and what made it even more thrilling was the knowledge that I would be working here if only for a short while. A smile spread across my face, stretching from ear to ear.

Once the plane came to a stop, we were parked well away from the terminal. I could see mobile stairs being driven across the apron, ground crew moving with purpose, and a couple of coaches approaching to transfer passengers from the aircraft to the terminal.

When the doors finally opened, and I gathered my things, I made my way toward the exit. And then it hit me, the smell, the warmth in the air, that unmistakable feeling that you have arrived overseas in a warm climate.

The flight attendants, as they're called now, smiled as passengers disembarked, and I joined the familiar ranks of package holidaymakers stepping off the aircraft.

The thrill of arriving was overwhelming. The warm air wrapped around me instantly, thick and alive, and in that moment, I felt completely enthralled by it. It wasn't just heat, it was possibility. Every breath carried excitement, a sense that something new was beginning, that I had stepped out of one life and into another. I stood there for a brief second, smiling to myself, knowing this was the start of something that would stay with me forever.

I couldn't help but laugh, letting out a quiet chuckle as I thought of my friends back in the UK, in Whitstable, probably enduring another dull, rainy day. I pictured the commuters heading into London, squeezed onto overcrowded tubes, faces fixed in routine and resignation. And here I was, yes, me, in Majorca, starting a new life.

I knew it wouldn't be forever. I understood even then that my time on the island was limited. But none of that mattered in that moment. What mattered was the feeling, the freedom, the excitement, the sheer disbelief that this was actually happening. Limited or not, this was extraordinary.

We crowded onto the buses for the short journey to the terminal. Almost immediately, I caught the unmistakable smell of someone with body odour and couldn't help thinking that surely a splash of Brut, Old Spice, or even the new one, Lynx, might have helped. But there was nothing I could do about it, so I endured it in silence.

The Spanish bus driver slammed the doors shut and took off at what felt like breakneck speed toward the terminal. Looking back through the window, I could see luggage being unloaded, bags thrown down from above by a couple of Spaniards in the aircraft's cargo hold, caught by two men below, and hurriedly stacked onto the back of a lorry.

I laughed to myself. It was all so wonderfully comical, like something straight out of Fawlty Towers. I couldn't imagine anything like it ever happening at a London airport.

As we entered the terminal, we were ushered toward passport control, then into the baggage reclaim area. It was there that I spotted my first overseas rep from the same company. I walked over and introduced myself. She smiled warmly and said she had been expecting me, and one other, on the flight, and told me to collect my bags and head for Coach D, bound for Palma Nova and Magaluf.

For the first time, I truly felt part of something. Someone special, even. I felt proud.

As I stood there, I noticed a young boy nudge his mum and whisper, "That's a rep too, Mum."

"Don't be silly," she replied. "He's just here on holiday like us."

But the boy knew. He'd heard. I caught his eye and gave him a small wink. The cheeky blighter grinned and gave me a thumbs-up in return. I've never forgotten that exact moment. It was a splendid feeling, being called a rep, and by a young lad no less. My first time overseas, officially being seen as one.

Overseas reps weren't what they are today. We were more than guides or customer service. We were a piece of home, a sense of security, a safety net. Someone to laugh with, drink with, confide in, flirt with, and sometimes fall for. I always thought of us as a kind of friendly British army abroad, scattered across sun-soaked resorts, quietly looking after our own.

As I walked through the terminal doors and finally escaped the chaos behind me, I saw the familiar line of company coaches waiting outside, all clearly labelled, each with a driver and a transfer representative standing at the front. I had once applied to be a transfer rep myself. I'd thought it looked like an incredible job, all the perks with far less trouble, but I hadn't been given that role. Instead, I'd landed something a little more high-bred. I was an overseas representative for short periods while also working in the UK office as part of a special programme. I cover that in more depth in my other book, Echoes in Andalusia.

I knew this stay in Majorca was only the beginning for me, and I couldn't wait to see where it would lead.

I dragged my case along the floor, one of those big, ugly old suitcases with a huge strap across the front and two more down the sides. No wheels, of course. You either found a trolley or you dragged it along like you were entering the World's Strongest Man competition.

When I finally reached Coach D, I smiled and offered my very first words in Spanish.

"Hola… I'm Wesley, here from the company."

The driver gave a simple nod. Then the transfer rep stepped forward and shook my hand. He was a lovely young lad called Daniel.

"Hola, Wesley! Good to see you, mate," he said cheerfully. "Chuck your bag down the side, Manuel will put it in the coach. Jump on board, and we'll have a chat on the way. It's not far anyway."

I dragged my case along the side of the coach, dropped it where he pointed, and climbed aboard. Inside, it smelled old and smoky, and looking around, I could see the seats were pure 1970s in design. I smiled to myself. This, too, was all part of the adventure.

The final few passengers boarded the coach and, once everyone was settled, Daniel picked up the microphone.

"Welcome to Palma de Mallorca," he said brightly, pausing before adding with a grin, "or as we British like to say, Palma in Majorca!"

A ripple of laughter moved through the coach.

"Right then," he continued. "We'll be making our way to the resorts now. We'll be driving briefly through the centre of

Palma city, so you'll catch a glimpse of the streets and the cathedral, before heading along the coast to Palma Nova and then Magaluf. Transfer time today is around thirty to forty minutes, traffic depending."

He glanced down at his notes.

"Our first hotel will be the Santa Lucia in Palma Nova. Weather-wise, you've picked a good week for this time of year. We've been averaging between eighteen and twenty-three degrees during the day, and the forecast looks mostly sunny with temperatures around twenty to twenty-four degrees. So, you should all enjoy yourselves."

With that, he put the microphone down and slid into the seat beside me.

"I've made your drop first," he said quietly. "The team leader's waiting to welcome you at the hotel, so I thought I'd get you in nice and quickly."

I smiled. "What's she like?"

"Oh, she's great fun," he replied. "You'll like her, I'm sure of it."

"You'll actually be staying at the hotel for the next month," Daniel said, lowering his voice slightly. "There's been a bit of a mix-up with the apartments, so you'll be sharing a room with someone else for now. But all your food's covered, and honestly, everyone's said that if you need anything at all, just give a shout, someone will always help."

He grinned.

"I reckon you're lucky, to be fair. You'll have a balcony and a decent view. Just hope you don't end up sharing with a snorer."

I laughed at that. I hated snorers, so I was very much hoping I wouldn't end up sharing with one.

"Do you know who I'll be sharing with?" I asked.

"Yeah," Daniel replied. "Some five-year rep flying in from Scotland in a couple of days. They reckon it'll work well for you; she can bring you up to speed."

He laughed again.

"Of course," he added, "that could mean many things. I joked in the meeting earlier that if Wesley's got a smile on his face all week, then we'll know he's definitely up to speed."

I nudged him playfully. "Oi! Don't start spreading things, you don't even know me!"

He burst out laughing, and I couldn't help but chuckle along with him. I liked Daniel already. He was a natural comedian and, more importantly, he had exactly my sense of humour.

The reality was that I was young, ambitious, yes, but inexperienced as a rep, and if I'm honest, inexperienced in life too. Not a virgin or anything like that, but certainly not a man of the world. So, the idea of sharing a room with a woman was not something I'd expected.

My mind immediately wandered to what my mum would say. I could picture it perfectly, the slight frown, the raised eyebrow, the unspoken concern written all over her face. I smiled to myself at the thought.

Then a far more practical worry struck me.

Oh God… what if I fart a lot?

Suddenly, the reality of it all hit me properly. I was about to share a room with a complete stranger, and in my eyes, a mature woman no less. The confidence I'd been feeling moments earlier wobbled slightly.

Oh, dear Lord, I thought. And just like that, I was starting to worry.

Chapter Two

As I arrived at the Hotel Santa Lucia, which sat right on the far end curve of the beach in Palma Nova, I was momentarily stopped in my tracks by its setting. The bay stretched out in front of the hotel, wide and calm, and for a few seconds I simply stood there beside my case, taking it all in.

Other passengers had already disembarked and were making their way inside, but I lingered, my eyes fixed on the beach below. It might have been shoulder season, but there were still people scattered along the sand, lying back and trying their best to catch a few precious rays of sunshine.

I remember thinking how perfect it all looked. And then, almost without realising it, my mind wandered further, imagining a small, clean, knee-high wave rolling gently into the bay. Even then, stupidly perhaps, I was already thinking what a fantastic spot it would be to surf… if only it had waves.

A voice called out from behind me.

"Hola, Señor Baker!"

I turned to see a lovely, short, rather plump woman smiling warmly in my direction. She had dark hair, kind eyes, and was dressed in a rep's uniform that she wore with easy confidence.

This must be Julia, I thought, the team leader.

I smiled and shook her hand, suddenly aware of my own nerves. She looked me up and down with a playful assessment and said, grinning, "So this is what London has sent me, then… you'll do, I suppose."

I laughed. "Well, actually, I'm a beach boy from a small harbour town in Kent, but yes, London has sent me."

She grinned back. "Good. Let's get you settled in, and then we'll have a proper chat about the office, routines, and what we've got planned for you."

As we started walking, I said, "I hear I'm sharing with a woman from Scotland who's flying over later this week."

She gave a small shake of her head. "Ahh, that was the plan until about an hour ago. Things have changed."

"Oh?" I said, suddenly alert.

"She's been sent to Ibiza instead," Julia explained. "A rep resigned at the end of her winter shift, so they're sending her in to help with the pre-season setup over there. You're on your own in the room now."

I felt a quiet wave of relief wash over me.

"And", she added, "we'll be splitting some of her duties between a few of the team, including you."

I glanced at Julia with a half-smile and said, jokingly, "I was rather looking forward to sharing with a woman, you know."

She stopped, turned to me slowly, and raised an eyebrow.

"Oh really?" she said, unimpressed but amused. "Well, don't get too comfortable. This is work first, fun second, if you're lucky."

She paused, then smiled.

"And besides," she added, "you've only just arrived. Let's see how you survive your first week before we worry about anything else."

I laughed, suitably put back in my place.

Julia led me through the hotel entrance and toward reception, exchanging quick words in Spanish with the staff as we passed. It all felt reassuringly efficient, as if I'd been quietly absorbed into a system that already knew what it was doing.

"We'll do a proper run-through shortly," she said, handing me a key. "But first, go and get yourself settled. Freshen up, have a look around, and then meet me in the bar downstairs in thirty minutes. We'll have a chat and ease you in."

"Perfect," I said, relieved to have a moment to myself.

She smiled. "Welcome to Majorca, Wes."

I thanked her and made my way toward the lift, dragging my suitcase behind me. The corridors were quiet, tiled in that unmistakable Spanish hotel style of marble that felt both dated and comforting at the same time. I found my room, slid the key into the door, and stepped inside.

The room was simple but clean, with twin beds neatly made, pale walls, and a small table by the window. I dropped my case, kicked off my shoes, and without even unpacking, walked straight toward the balcony doors.

I pulled them open and stepped outside.

The view stopped me in my tracks.

Palma Nova bay stretched out in front of me, calm and inviting, the sea catching the light in soft shades of blue and silver. The curve of the beach led my eye gently along the coastline toward Magaluf in the distance, quiet for now, waiting for the season to wake it properly.

I leaned on the balcony rail and just stood there, breathing it in. The air was warm, the kind of warmth that settles on your skin rather than presses against it. Below, people strolled along the promenade, unhurried, as if time had agreed to move a little slower here.

For a moment, everything went quiet inside my head.

This was real. I was here. Not visiting. Not passing through. Living.

I glanced at my watch, realised I had just enough time, and smiled. Thirty minutes. A new place, a new job, a new version of life waiting downstairs in the bar.

I turned back into the room, already knowing I was going to like it here.

After unpacking and settling in, it was time to head back downstairs to meet Julia. I glanced at my watch and realised I was cutting it fine. The lift, of course, took an age to arrive, but eventually it did, whisking me back down toward the bar.

Julia was already there, sitting at a small table, and as I approached, I noticed a tall glass of cola waiting for me.

"I thought you'd like that," she said.

I nodded, smiling, and thanked her. It was a small gesture, but I appreciated it.

She began outlining the plan for my first few days. The initial focus would be orientation, getting to know the hotels in the area, along with the nearby apartment blocks. She'd set aside a specific task for me: checking disabled facilities across the properties. Everything from ramps at hotel entrances, to door widths, and whether a wheelchair could comfortably fit inside the bathrooms of designated disabled rooms.

It was detailed, practical work, and I liked that straight away.

Once that was completed, she explained, I'd start sharing responsibility for a few hotels, and we'd see how things progressed from there. She also mentioned that a contracts manager would be visiting soon to oversee contracting for the following season, and that I'd be joining him during his stay. The thought of that immediately appealed to me. I was genuinely looking forward to meeting the wider team and getting properly stuck in.

Before we finished, Julia added one last piece of information.

"The room next to yours is occupied by female reps also working Palma Nova," she said. "The rest of the team is staying in an apartment about five minutes' walk away; they're covering Magaluf."

I felt a flicker of excitement at that. New colleagues, new neighbours, a whole new world beginning to take shape.

And with that, Julia stood up and gathered her things. Just as she was about to leave, she paused and turned back to me.

"One word of warning," she said quietly. "Watch out for Tim. He's pleasant enough to your face, but he's got a reputation for stirring and gossiping. Best to keep yourself to yourself around him; he's caused a few issues in the past."

I nodded, taking it in.

With that, she walked off with a confident little swagger, leaving me sitting there, glass in hand, suddenly contemplating the reality of it all.

Even here, on the sunny island of Mallorca, it seemed that idiots could still find a way to spoil things.

I could hear the low hum of conversation around the bar and began to recognise a few familiar faces, people I'd seen earlier on the plane and then again on the coach. One of them caught my eye and smiled, and I smiled back.

And then I spotted him.

The little lad from the airport.

He was sitting with his mum and dad a few tables away and, when he noticed me looking, he broke into a wide grin. I smiled to myself. Bless him, I thought. Tomorrow, when he sees me in my uniform, his mum will owe him an apology.

Then I glanced at her and immediately realised how unlikely that was.

I chuckled quietly into my drink before catching myself. That was unfair. Judging people by how they look, assigning character without knowing anything about them, wasn't right. I gave myself a silent telling-off and let the thought drift away.

Some lessons, it seemed, started early.

Chapter Three

After my first evening meal in the hotel, I put on a decent shirt and a jumper and headed out for a walk. Nothing planned, I just wanted to get a feel for the area, to see what Palma Nova looked like once the light had faded.

A handful of bars were open, quiet but welcoming, their doors spilling warm yellow light onto the pavement. At one point, a man approached me offering weed, or something stronger, no doubt. Drugs had never been my thing, so I brushed him off quickly, though I was slightly shocked to see it even during shoulder season.

After about an hour of wandering aimlessly through the streets, I headed back to the hotel. I went up to my room and stood for a moment on the balcony, looking across the bay at the lights twinkling softly on the water. It felt calm. Settling.

I decided to grab a shower.

Not long after, I realised I wasn't as alone as I thought.

Fresh from the shower, I was lying on the bed in my pyjamas, flicking through the Britannia in-flight magazine I'd taken earlier, when I heard a bit of commotion outside on the balcony. A couple of giggles. Then a voice.

"Come on, he's awake, he's on his bed."

To my horror, two women suddenly appeared, climbing in from the balcony.

A woman stepped forward, smiling broadly. "Hi! I'm Stephanie, and this is Alison. We're your fellow reps here in Palma Nova."

I stared at them, half-laughing, half-stunned. "Have you just climbed around the balcony wall?"

They both burst into giggles.

"Well, we did knock earlier," Stephanie said, "but you didn't answer. And we knew you were in., so we just swung our legs around the wall and pulled ourselves onto your balcony"

"I was in the shower," I replied.

"Ohhh," Alison said, nodding. "That explains it."

They wandered in as if this were the most normal thing in the world.

"So," Stephanie said, looking me over, "how are you? And where are you from?"

I was still in mild shock, but to be honest, I found the whole thing bloody hilarious.

"Kent," I said. "Near Canterbury. A small coastal town you might never of heard of called Whitstable."

They exchanged looks.

"I'm from Skegness," Stephanie said proudly.

"And I'm from Nottingham," Alison added.

"Northern girls, then?" I smiled.

"Yep," Stephanie grinned. "Through and through. That's us."

They both made themselves comfortable without asking. Alison perched on the edge of the spare bed while Stephanie leaned against the dressing table, arms folded, clearly taking everything in.

"So," Stephanie said, glancing around the room, "what do you think so far?"

"I've been here a few hours," I replied. "So far I've unpacked, had dinner, gone for a walk, been offered drugs, and had two women climb into my room via the balcony."

She laughed. "Sounds about right."

Alison grinned. "Welcome to rep life."

I shook my head, still smiling. "Do you always enter rooms like that?"

"Only when the door doesn't get answered," Stephanie said matter-of-factly. "You'll learn quickly, knocking is optional around here."

"That's reassuring," I said. "I'll sleep with one eye open."

She laughed again. "You'll get used to it. There's not much privacy once the season gets going. We're all in and out of each other's rooms constantly, or if you are in the apartments, then you probably get a bit more privacy."

"And besides," Alison added, "we wanted to meet you properly. Julia said you were arriving today."

"Ah," I said. "So, this is an inspection."

"Something like that," Stephanie replied, smiling. "We had to see what London had sent us."

I raised an eyebrow. "And?"

She pretended to think for a moment. "You'll do. For now."

We all laughed.

"So," Alison said, leaning back on her hands, "what's your background then? First season?"

"Well, it is my first proper overseas stint," I replied. "I've done bits and pieces before, but nothing like this. I have been in the head office a lot prior to this and will be going back, I understand"

Stephanie nodded. "You'll be fine. Palma Nova's a good place to learn, busy enough, but not insane. That comes later. Will you be here all the season?"

"In Magaluf, that is crazy in summer" Alison added knowingly.

"I've heard, and no, I don't think I am here for the full season, Stephanie", I said.

Stephanie smiled. "You will enjoy life here; we will make you have fun."

There was a brief pause, the easy kind, not awkward, just unhurried.

"Come on," Stephanie said suddenly, pushing herself upright. "We're heading downstairs for a drink. You're not getting away with an early night on your first evening."

I glanced down at my pyjamas. "I'm not exactly dressed for public consumption in the bar."

"That's your problem," Alison laughed. "You've got five minutes to get ready."

They both turned and walked out the room by the door this time as casually as they'd arrived.

"We'll meet you in the bar," Stephanie called over her shoulder. "And Wesley?"

"Yes?"

She grinned. "Lock your balcony door next time."

I stood there for a moment, shaking my head, still smiling to myself.

It was becoming very clear that this was not going to be a quiet season.

I got changed as quickly as I could, but then, being mischievous by nature, I decided I wasn't about to let that balcony entrance go unanswered.

I stepped back outside and glanced along the row of balconies. Sure enough, I could see straight into their room. The balcony door was wide open.

Perfect.

I grabbed my room key, climbed around the wall divide, and swung myself neatly onto their balcony. Slipping inside, I took a quick look around. The room was identical to mine, with twin beds and simple furniture, and I immediately noticed what I'd already spotted when unpacking: wooden slats supporting the mattresses.

An idea formed instantly.

I went to one of the beds, lifted the mattress carefully, and quietly slid out lots of the wooden slats. I then tucked them neatly under the other bed, completely out of sight, before placing the mattress back exactly as it had been.

Whoever lay on that bed later was in for a surprise.

Satisfied with my work, I checked my watch. About ten minutes had passed, perfect timing. I walked out the door this time and headed downstairs to the bar, doing my best to look innocent.

Now, I thought, let's see how they enjoy my sense of humour.

The girls had already bought me a drink by the time I arrived, a Bacardi and Coke, and it went down a treat. The measures in Spain, or anywhere else in Europe, for that matter, were nothing like back home. In the UK, everything was poured with military precision; here, the barman simply free-poured whatever felt right. It was dangerously easy to get used to.

Stephanie was exactly as she had seemed earlier, bubbly, confident, and full of energy. She had striking blue eyes, curly blonde hair, and a presence that naturally drew attention. I imagined she was well noticed by tourists and locals alike, and she wore that attention easily, without trying.

Alison was different. She had short, dark hair cut into a neat bob, kind eyes, and a softer, more grounded way about her. There was something reassuring in how she spoke and listened, something quietly caring. I found myself liking her almost immediately; she intrigued me.

As we sat there talking and laughing, it dawned on me just how new I was to all of this. Overseas life. Rep life. The unspoken rules and rhythms. I was innocent, really, eager, curious, and completely unseasoned.

And I could already tell that, to these two, I was fresh bait.

Alison looked at me thoughtfully for a moment before smiling. "I think you're going to have a lot of fun here," she said. "And honestly, we're really glad to have a man join the team. Last year it was just us girls, and sometimes having a bloke around helps with… awkward people."

I laughed. "So, you've both worked here before, then?"

"Oh yes," she replied. "This is our third season in Mallorca. Stephanie did Ibiza before coming here, and we both head to the Canary Islands in winter."

Stephanie nodded. "We've been pretty lucky, actually. We seem to get placed together a lot."

"I reckon that's because we're good," Alison added with a grin. "Excursions, guest relations, all that stuff."

Stephanie turned back to me. "You'll mainly be covering the Palma Nova properties, Wes. Though I think you might have one place over in Magaluf as well with us."

She took a sip of her drink. "But we'll be sharing most of the units between us anyway, so it should work really well."

I nodded, taking it all in, the places, the seasons, the rhythm of it all. It was suddenly very clear that these two knew exactly what they were doing.

And I was just getting started.

"I'll be honest," I said after a moment, lowering my voice slightly. "I'm a bit nervous. I know my stuff, but it's daunting. I feel like I've been beamed into a completely different world. I'm not complaining, not at all, but I know I'll have to catch up quickly."

Alison looked at me thoughtfully while Stephanie burst out laughing.

"Wesley," Alison said gently, "I can already tell you'll be fine. In fact, probably better than fine. You're very grounded for a new rep. And honestly, you're calm, I mean, we climbed into your bedroom, and you didn't bat an eyelid. You were just lying there in pyjamas that looked like they came straight out of the 1970s."

She paused, then smiled mischievously.

"Seriously, Wes… where on earth did you get those? Your dad's wardrobe?"

I laughed. "I'm a man of distinction," I said proudly. "But actually, my mum packed them. I normally wear shorts and a T-shirt, she just said they looked comfortable."

Stephanie shook her head, laughing. "Well, they're certainly a turn-off for women, Wesley. You might want to ditch them."

I laughed, then added, half-joking, "So you think I'm going to be getting laid a lot, then?"

Alison replied without missing a beat. "It's not about whether you want to. You'll find it quite hard to avoid in this resort."

The two of them laughed and nudged each other, clearly enjoying themselves.

I took a sip of my drink, shaking my head slightly. Holy crap, I thought. Where am I? I couldn't help but picture my friends back home, and what they'd be thinking if they could see me now.

As we made our way upstairs later that night, I said goodnight to them both, completely forgetting the little joke I'd set up earlier in the other room.

Back in my own room, I lay down on the bed fully clothed, replaying the evening in my head. The conversations, the laughter, the sense of being suddenly dropped into a new life. Through the open balcony doors, I could hear the girls next door chatting and laughing as they got ready for bed.

Then came an almighty scream.

It was immediately followed by hysterical laughter.

Then a string of profanity words followed, most of it involving my name.

Moments later, there was loud knocking at my door.

I walked over as innocently as I could manage and opened it.

Standing there was Stephanie, laughing so hard she could barely speak. "Did you destroy Alison's bed?"

"Me?" I said, doing my best impression of shock. "I'm innocent. What's happened?"

"Oh come on," she laughed. "We know it was you, Wesley, you bloody prankster. We did not see that coming. Alison went straight through the bed. Her legs were pointing at the ceiling and fully open wide!"

I burst out laughing. "Alright, alright, I'll come and sort it."

I followed her next door to find Alison still half-tangled in the remains of the bed, swearing enthusiastically and laughing at the same time. Between the drinks and the shock, neither of them was exactly steady on their feet.

I helped Alison out, gathered up the missing wooden slats, and fixed the bed. Once she was back on solid ground, she pushed me playfully against the wall.

"You absolute idiot," she said, firing off several swear words, before bursting out laughing again.

Stephanie shook her head. "Bloody hell, Wesley. You've only just arrived and you're already causing trouble. Wait until the rest of the team hears about this tomorrow in the office."

Alison straightened herself up, walked over, and gave me a hug, followed by a big kiss on the cheek. "I could eat you alive!"

I won't lie. I rather enjoyed that, and the thought. On that note, I made my way out of the bedroom and gave a little chuckle to myself - that got them!

I awoke to what, in my relatively untravelled experience at the time, could only be described as paradise perfected. A beautiful stretch of golden sand, an aqua-coloured sea, and warm sunlight spilling through the window.

I laughed out loud.

"Bloody hell," I said to myself. "I'm really here. This is my life. This is my career."

I put on my uniform and headed downstairs for breakfast, feeling absurdly proud. There I was, an overseas rep at last. The uniform actually looked good on me, and as I walked into the restaurant, the head waiter greeted me with a nod and a smile that made it all feel even more real.

At the far table, I spotted the girls. They waved me over, and I joined them, still grinning like an idiot.

Breakfast was a buffet, and I made the most of it, bacon, eggs, baked beans, then went back for the continental option too, piling on ham, cheese, and fresh bread rolls. It felt indulgent and exciting all at once.

This was magic. Real magic.

"So," I asked between mouthfuls, "what are we all up to today?"

They talked me through their plans, and then Stephanie ran through what she knew of mine, exactly as Julia had explained the night before. Hotel visits, orientation, and getting familiar with the area.

I listened, nodding along, excitement building with every sentence.

I was ready to get started.

Just across the restaurant, I spotted the little lad from the airport. As soon as he saw me in my uniform, his face lit up, and he gave me an enthusiastic wave.

I waved back.

He immediately nudged his mum, animatedly whispering something in her ear. I could almost read his lips.

I told you he was…

Alison noticed and looked at me curiously. "Do you know that boy and his family already?"

"No," I said, smiling. "But we had a bit of an exchange of looks at the airport. He told his mum I was a rep, but she didn't believe him."

I glanced back over. The boy was still grinning proudly.

"I think he's just putting her straight now."

Alison laughed softly. "How sweet."

I finished my coffee and asked, "So who's doing the welcome meeting here today?"

Stephanie shook her head. "None of us, including you, Wes. This isn't our hotel. Joanna and Pauline look after this one."

That surprised me, but also quietly pleased me.

It meant, at least for today, we were safe from being hunted down by unhappy guests. It also meant I needed to quickly get up to speed on what my duties would be and where.

Being an overseas representative is really tough work, and I knew that I was in for a lot of fun but an awful lot of really testing and difficult times as well.

Finishing breakfast I called Julia to find out my first tasks then next to my room to collect my reps briefcase, albeit the day ahead was in the office.

Chapter Four

On the second day, before I began learning the job properly, I found myself once again drawn to the balcony.

From up there, the curve of Palma Nova bay seemed almost too perfect to be real. The sand stretched in a soft golden arc, hugging the shoreline as the sea lapped in gentle, rhythmic waves. The water was a clear, shifting blend of turquoise and deeper blues, the kind of colour you only ever saw in travel brochures, and yet here it was, moving and glinting under the morning sun.

To the right, the coastline drifted toward Magaluf, still quiet at that hour, as if waiting patiently for the season to wake it fully. The promenade below traced the edge of the beach in a neat line, palm trees standing like quiet sentries, their shadows long and lazy against the pavement.

Small fishing boats rocked softly in the distance. A couple of early swimmers cut clean lines through the water. Somewhere nearby, crockery clinked from a café preparing for the day. It was peaceful, almost deceptively so.

It struck me then how easy it would be to mistake this place for a holiday. To see only the colours, the warmth, the gentle sea, and forget that behind every sunbed and balcony door were expectations. Questions. Complaints. Responsibility.

I leaned on the rail and took one last deep breath of the warm air.

This wasn't a postcard.

This was my office.

And it was time to learn how to work in it.

I dressed more carefully that morning, smoothing down the uniform shirt as if it carried more weight than fabric alone. There was something about wearing it properly for the first full working day, not just to look the part, but to begin feeling it.

Julia had told me which hotel to start with and the time. It was only a short walk along the promenade, and I set off with a clipboard tucked under my arm and my red coloured rep briefcase, trying to look as though I had been doing this for years.

The bay was still calm, the light brighter now, tourists already claiming their chosen sunbeds with towels draped possessively across them. A few nodded as I passed, some glancing at the badge on my shirt. The shift was subtle but unmistakable. I was no longer just another young man wandering through the resort. I was someone they might ask for help.

That thought both thrilled and unsettled me.

The hotel entrance was cool and shaded compared to the warmth outside. Inside, the reception area carried that familiar holiday smell, polished floors, air conditioning, and faint sun cream. I paused for a moment, taking in the layout, noticing the ramp near the entrance, the width of the doorway, the positioning of the lift.

Right, I told myself. This is where it starts.

The receptionist looked up and smiled politely.

"Buenos días."

"Buenos días," I replied, hoping my accent didn't betray too much. "I'm Wesley."

She nodded as though this was perfectly ordinary, though to me it felt monumental.

"Ah yes. Julia mentioned you. Welcome."

That small sentence settled me more than she could have known.

I began my hotel and bedroom checks methodically. Ramps first, were they practical, not just decorative? Door widths, would a wheelchair genuinely fit through? Bathroom access, could someone manoeuvre comfortably without feeling confined?

It wasn't glamorous. There were no cheering crowds, no dramatic rescues, no stories to retell at the bar. Just quiet, careful observation.

And yet, I found myself oddly satisfied.

This was trust.

This was being useful.

This was the part of the job most guests never saw but relied upon completely.

By the time I finished the first hotel, the clipboard felt less like a prop and more like a tool. I stepped back out into the sunlight, blinking slightly, aware that something subtle had shifted.

I hadn't just arrived in Mallorca.

I had started working in it.

I left the first hotel feeling steadier than when I had entered it. The sun was higher now, the promenade beginning to hum with life. Families were drifting towards the beach, elderly couples walked arm in arm, and a few early sun worshippers had already claimed prime positions near the water.

Clipboard tucked under my arm once more; I headed toward the next property on my list. It was slightly further along the bay, past a small row of souvenir shops and a café where an elderly Spanish man was carefully arranging chairs outside, lining them up with quiet precision.

The second hotel was larger and busier, even in the shoulder season. I paused outside for a moment, studying the entrance. No obvious ramp. A small step. My mind began to tick over automatically now.

Inside, I introduced myself again, this time with a little more ease.

"Good morning, I'm Wesley,"

The words came more smoothly now. Less rehearsed.

The receptionist gave me a measured look, not unfriendly, but assessing. Reps, I was beginning to realise, had to earn their place with hotel staff. They had seen many come and go. Some helpful. Some not.

I asked about disabled rooms. Lift access. Emergency procedures. I made notes carefully, checking corridors, counting steps, and measuring spaces with my stride when I didn't have a tape measure to hand.

There was something quietly grounding about it all. This wasn't glamour. This was detail. And detail, I was learning, was what prevented problems later.

By mid-afternoon, I had visited three properties. My shirt clung slightly to my back in the warmth, and my once-perfectly smoothed hair had surrendered to the Mediterranean air.

I stopped briefly by the beach before heading back to the Santa Lucia. The bay shimmered again, tourists laughing, a speedboat cutting a white line across the blue. It looked effortless.

But my day had not been effortless.

It had been steady. Careful. Responsible.

Back at the hotel, I headed straight to the small back office area that Julia had shown me before. It wasn't glamorous, a desk, a telephone, a slightly temperamental fax machine, and a stack of headed paper with the company logo printed proudly across the top.

I rewrote my notes clearly onto the official information sheets: ramp gradients, doorway widths, bathroom access, and lift sizes. No scribbles now. This would be read by the customer service team and the reservations department back in London. Decisions would be made based on what I wrote.

That thought made me sit a little straighter.

When I finished, I fed the sheets into the fax machine one by one. It whirred, clicked, and then began its strange mechanical song, the high-pitched electronic tones travelling through invisible lines back to the head office.

London.

It suddenly felt very far away.

The final sheet slid through, and I waited for the confirmation tone. When it came, I felt an unexpected wave of satisfaction.

It wasn't dramatic.

No one applauded.

But somewhere in an office in the UK, someone would shortly receive those pages and update files because of me.

I leaned back in the chair and allowed myself a small smile.

I wasn't just in Mallorca.

I was part of the machine now.

And for the first time that day, I truly felt like a representative.

A few days later, I found myself working from a hotel set slightly back from the bay. You could still smell the sea from the entrance, but the view was mostly rooftops and the tops of palm trees rather than open water.

By then, I had found a rhythm to the mornings, checking the noticeboard, updating excursion sheets, making sure my contact times were clear. I was just finishing a brief conversation with reception when I noticed a couple standing nearby, watching me intently.

They were waiting.

The man approached first, mid-forties perhaps, broad Nottingham accent, already flushed slightly with irritation.

"You the rep then?"

"Yes," I replied, offering a steady smile. "Wesley. How can I help?"

His wife stepped forward quickly.

"We've got a problem."

I gestured towards a quieter corner of the lobby.

"Let's have a chat."

The complaints came in quick succession.

They had paid for a sea view, or at least believed they had, and were facing the rear of the hotel. The beds were uncomfortable. The staff, in their view, were unfriendly. And the resort itself was "dead."

"We were expecting a bit of life," the husband said sharply. "Not this."

I listened. Properly listened. That was something Julia had emphasised, let them empty the tank first.

When they paused for breath, the wife added, "We feel like we've been mis-sold."

The word hung there.

That was the moment I felt the weight of the badge on my shirt.

I asked calmly, "May I see your booking confirmation?"

The husband sighed theatrically but handed over the paperwork. I scanned it carefully. Standard room. No guaranteed sea view listed.

"I can see here," I said gently, "that this booking is for a standard room. Sea views are listed as a supplement, and I'm afraid they're subject to availability."

"That's not what we were told," he snapped.

"I understand it's frustrating," I replied evenly. "Let me speak to reception and see if there's anything we can do."

They continued, now turning their frustration toward the company itself. Comments about being "ripped off" and "never booking with us again." The tone edged toward abusive.

I kept my voice level.

"I'm here to help," I said calmly. "Shouting won't speed it up. Let's see what options we have."

It was the first time I had consciously steadied my own breathing in a professional setting.

I spoke to reception. There were limited sea-view rooms available, but one was due to become vacant the following morning. It would require a small supplement, but I asked whether that could be waived as a goodwill gesture. After some negotiation, they agreed to a reduced rate for the upgrade.

I returned to the couple.

"There's a sea-view room available tomorrow," I explained. "I've managed to reduce the upgrade cost significantly. In the meantime, I've arranged a couple of complimentary drinks vouchers for you at the bar this evening."

They looked at each other.

"And the beds?" the wife asked.

"I've requested maintenance to check the mattresses today," I said. "If needed, we'll have them changed."

There was a pause.

"And the resort?" the husband said more quietly now.

"This is shoulder season," I replied honestly. "Palma Nova is lively in summer. At this time of year, some bars operate reduced hours. There are still a few busier spots I can recommend tonight, but it won't be peak-season energy."

I watched them absorb that.

"I'd rather be upfront with you," I added. "This time of year suits some guests perfectly; others prefer the high season."

The edge had softened now.

They weren't smiling, but they weren't shouting either.

"Alright," the husband muttered. "We'll see how tomorrow goes."

When they walked away, I felt something shift inside me.

Not relief.

Competence.

It hadn't been glamorous. They hadn't thanked me profusely. But I had taken a situation that was heating up and cooled it.

I stood in the lobby for a moment longer than necessary, letting my pulse settle.

Being a rep wasn't about the sunsets or the Bacardi measures.

It was about absorbing impact without reflecting it.

And that, I was learning, took far more skill than I had imagined.

The next morning dawned even brighter than the last.

The sky was a clear, endless blue, not a cloud daring to interrupt it. The bay lay almost perfectly still, the surface of the water smooth and glass-like, reflecting the light in soft, shimmering ripples. The warmth had edged up a degree or two, and there was a subtle hum in the air that hadn't been there before, as though the season itself was slowly waking.

I stepped out onto the promenade early, before most guests had finished breakfast. The sea carried that clean, salty scent, and a gentle breeze moved through the palms overhead. Somewhere nearby, a café machine hissed into life, and the rhythmic sound of someone sweeping sand from a terrace drifted across the morning.

Walking along the bay that day, clipboard in hand once more, I felt strangely buoyant.

Alive.

It struck me how fortunate I was to be walking to work beside turquoise water, to have the sun warming my back instead of grey skies pressing down. Even the simple act of crossing the promenade felt purposeful now. I wasn't wandering anymore.

I was going somewhere.

As I approached the hotel set back from the beach, I could already see the couple from Nottingham standing near reception, their suitcases positioned neatly beside them. The tension from the previous day had softened; they looked expectant rather than combative.

"Morning," I said, offering a calm smile.

The husband nodded. "Morning."

Reception confirmed that the sea-view room was ready. I accompanied them upstairs, key in hand, wanting to see the resolution through properly.

When the door opened, the room immediately felt brighter. The curtains were drawn back, and through the glass balcony doors, the bay stretched out in full view, sunlight catching the water in sharp flashes of silver and blue.

The wife stepped forward first.

"Well," she said quietly, "that's more like it."

The husband walked onto the balcony, leaned on the rail, and looked out across the water.

"Yeah," he admitted. "That's what we had in mind."

I explained the reduced supplement again and confirmed that the drink vouchers had been credited the previous evening. Maintenance had also replaced the mattresses in their original room, not that they would now need them.

There was a small pause.

"Thanks for sorting it," the wife said eventually.

It wasn't overly warm. It wasn't effusive. But it was genuine.

"That's what I'm here for," I replied.

As I left them to unpack, I felt a quiet satisfaction settle over me. Not triumph. Not relief.

Balance.

I had seen the problem through from agitation to acceptance. No miracles. No drama. Just steady handling.

Back out on the promenade, the sun had climbed higher, and the bay looked almost impossibly beautiful. A few more loungers were filling now, children's laughter echoing faintly from the water's edge.

I walked slowly for a moment before heading toward my next property.

The island hadn't changed overnight.

But I had.

That evening, the three of us found ourselves back in the hotel bar.

The sun had long dipped behind the buildings, but the warmth still lingered in the air. The terrace doors were open, and the low hum of holiday conversation drifted in from outside. Glasses clinked. Someone laughed too loudly at a joke that probably wasn't that funny. The usual soundtrack of a resort easing into the night.

Stephanie was already halfway through a Bacardi and Coke when I arrived.

"Well?" she said, raising an eyebrow. "How did Nottingham go?"

I sat down slowly, letting out a breath I hadn't realised I'd been holding all week.

"Sea view secured," I said. "Reduced supplement. Beds changed. Drink vouchers deployed."

Alison grinned. "Look at you."

"They weren't easy," I admitted. "Started off… aggressive."

Stephanie nodded knowingly. "They always do. Especially when they think they've been mis-sold."

"I thought they were going to explode at one point," I said. "They had a go at the company. At the hotel. At me."

"And you didn't lose it?" Alison asked.

"No," I said. "I just… slowed down. Let them talk. Then dealt with it."

Stephanie leaned back in her chair. "That's the trick. You absorb it. You don't bounce it back."

There was something comforting about hearing that from someone more experienced. It meant I hadn't just survived the situation, I'd handled it correctly.

The conversation drifted into other stories. Stephanie had dealt with a guest who had locked themselves out on the balcony. Alison had calmed down a family arguing over excursion pick-up times.

We compared notes. Laughed. Mocked the absurdity of certain complaints. Shared small victories.

At one point, Alison looked at me and said, "You've changed this week."

"Have I?" I replied.

"You're standing differently," she said. "More sure of yourself."

Stephanie nodded. "Less wide-eyed."

I laughed. "It's only been a few days."

"That's all it takes," Stephanie said. "This job either eats you or sharpens you. You're sharpening."

I took a slow sip of my drink and looked around the bar.

The guests chatting comfortably. The staff moving efficiently behind the counter. The soft glow of lights reflecting in the windows. Outside, beyond the dark outline of the bay, the Mediterranean rolled on as it always had.

A week ago, I had been looking at this place as a visitor.

Now I was part of the structure that made it function.

Tired, yes.

But alive.

And for the first time, I wasn't wondering whether I belonged here.

I knew I did.

Chapter Five

It's hard to properly explain to anyone who has never been an overseas representative what it felt like to stand up in front of a room full of holidaymakers and begin speaking.

On the surface, it was simple enough. A welcome meeting. A microphone. A handful of chairs. A group of people in shorts and sandals or flip flops who had only landed hours earlier.

But at the time, it felt enormous.

For many of them, this was their first time abroad. For others, maybe their second or third. Spain in the 1980s was not as casual as it feels today. There was still a sense of distance from home, a feeling that once you stepped off that plane, you were somewhere truly different.

And in that room, whether I realised it fully or not, I represented control.

They looked at you differently. Not as a fellow traveller. Not as another young Brit enjoying the sun. They looked at you as the one who knew what was going on. The one who could fix things. The one who would make sense of the unfamiliar.

Sure, they were on holiday.

But I was the constant.

Most of them didn't speak a word of Spanish. That alone was enough to unsettle people. Add to that a different currency, unfamiliar food, hotel staff speaking rapidly in another language, different customs, different ways of doing things, and suddenly the confident Brit abroad could feel like a slightly lost sheep.

And that's where we came in.

Our job wasn't just to tell them excursion times or emergency numbers. It was to remove fear without ever mentioning it. To make the foreign feel friendly. To smooth the edges of uncertainty so they could relax properly.

We were there to ensure none of those differences mattered.

So they could rest.
So they could laugh.
So they could lie in the sun without a single practical worry tugging at the back of their mind.

Standing up in front of that room for the first time, I understood something quietly but clearly.

This wasn't about talking.

It was about reassurance.

And whether I felt fully ready or not… they believed I was.

That all sounds very noble and well put together now.

At the time, I was mostly just trying not to look terrified.

I remember standing just outside the room before my first welcome meeting. I had my notes in one hand and what I hoped was a confident expression on my face. Inside, I could hear the low hum of holiday chatter, chairs scraping, glasses clinking, someone coughing theatrically as though preparing to judge my performance.

My heart was thumping harder than it had any right to.

It wasn't that I didn't know the information. I did. Emergency numbers. Excursions. Currency. Safety. Local tips. I'd read it all. Rehearsed it. Probably over-rehearsed it.

But knowing something and standing up to deliver it are two entirely different experiences.

When I finally walked in, every head turned.

That's the part no one warns you about.

Twenty, maybe thirty pairs of eyes lifting in unison. Some warm. Some curious. A couple mildly suspicious. One gentleman was already leaning back in his chair with arms folded as if to say, "Go on then, impress me."

I introduced myself.

The first few sentences came out slightly quicker than planned. Not incomprehensible, just… brisk. I distinctly remember thinking, Slow down, Wesley. You're not commentating on the Grand National or FA Cup final.

Somewhere near the front, a child whispered loudly, "Mum, he looks young."

That did wonders for my authority.

I smiled anyway. You learn quickly that smiling buys you time.

As I moved through the basics, something interesting began to happen. The room softened. People started nodding. A few wrote things down. One lady leaned forward instead of back. The folded-arm gentleman relaxed by about two inches.

They weren't there to catch me out.

They were there to feel safe.

I threw in a small joke about Spanish timekeeping, that "manana" didn't always mean tomorrow in the strict British sense of the word, and a ripple of laughter moved across the room. Nothing dramatic, but enough.

That laugh settled me more than any training ever could.

Halfway through, a hand went up.

Here we go, I thought. The test.

"Yes?"

"Is it true the locals don't like the English?"

It wasn't the question I expected, but there it was.

I paused for a second, just long enough not to look flustered.

"The locals," I said evenly, "like polite visitors who make an effort and enjoy plus respect the area."

There was a small murmur of agreement.

"And if you learn two or three Spanish words," I added, "you'll be amazed how much warmer the welcome becomes."

That seemed to land well.

From that moment on, I felt it, a subtle shift. Not dominance. Not performance. Just balance.

By the time I reached the end, I wasn't gripping my notes anymore. I was talking to them rather than at them.

"Most importantly," I said, finishing up, "this is your holiday. I'm here to make sure you enjoy it. If you need anything at all, don't sit and worry. Come and find me."

And I meant it.

As they filtered out, a few stopped to say thank you. One gentleman shook my hand. A lady asked about an excursion. The suspicious one gave me a short nod, which I took as a victory of the highest order.

When the room was empty, I exhaled properly for the first time in twenty minutes.

I hadn't fainted.
I hadn't forgotten anything crucial.
And nobody had tried to publicly dismantle me.

It may have seemed routine to anyone watching.

To me, it felt like crossing a threshold.

I had walked in hoping not to fail.

I walked out knowing I could do it.

And that made all the difference.

Of course, I'm fairly certain the glasses of sangria being handed out throughout the room helped things along rather nicely.

The British have always enjoyed a drink, and at ten o'clock in the morning, on the first full day of sunshine, it seemed to hit the spot. There's something about a glass of slightly over-sweet sangria that softens an audience. Shoulders drop. Smiles appear more easily. Questions feel less like interrogations and more like polite enquiries.

I'm not saying it was the reason the meeting went well.

But I'm not saying it wasn't.

As the last of the guests drifted out, clutching their leaflets and finishing their drinks, I gathered my notes and allowed myself a slow exhale. Not a dramatic one. Just enough to reset my lungs.

And that's when I saw her.

Julia had been standing at the back the entire time.

I genuinely hadn't noticed her come in. She'd positioned herself near the wall, arms folded, quietly observing. Watching. Assessing.

Which, in hindsight, made perfect sense.

She waited until the room was empty before walking towards me.

"Well done," she said simply.

There was a pause. The kind where you're not quite sure if that's the full sentence or merely the opening line.

"I thought you might have a bad time of it," she continued, studying me with that calm, measuring look she had. "A few people weren't sure what to expect."

I raised an eyebrow. "Oh?"

She nodded slightly.

"Some thought you might be a bit… wild."

That made me laugh. Apparently, I had developed a reputation before I'd even fully begun.

"But you're not," she said. "You're calm. Natural. You don't flap."

She tilted her head just slightly, as though she was still deciding something.

"I think you're something different, Wesley. I think you break the mould a little, don't you?"

It wasn't flattery. It was observation.

And it landed.

I didn't have a clever reply prepared. I wasn't trying to break any mould. I was just trying not to drop the microphone.

"I'm just trying to do it properly," I said.

She smiled that small, knowing smile.

"Keep doing that," she replied. "Guests feel it."

And with that, she turned and left the room.

I stood there for a moment longer than necessary, holding my clipboard, replaying her words in my head.

Break the mould.

At the time, I wasn't entirely sure what mould I was meant to be breaking. I wasn't the loudest rep. I wasn't theatrical. I wasn't the one dominating the bar at night.

But perhaps that was the point.

Some reps dazzled.

Some entertained.

Some bulldozed.

I steadied.

And in that quiet, slightly sticky room that still smelled faintly of sangria and sun cream, I realised something important.

You don't have to be the loudest person in the room to hold it.

You just have to be the calmest.

There was, however, no time to bask in quiet self-congratulation.

Because barely twenty minutes later, I was walking up the road to do it all again.

And not just once.

Three times.

Different unit. Different guests. Same sun. Same uniform. Same expectation in their eyes that I would somehow make everything clear, calm and manageable.

The first meeting had been nerve-wracking.

The second was physically harder.

By the time I arrived at the next hotel, the Mediterranean heat had risen properly. The promenade shimmered slightly, and my once-crisp shirt was already beginning to cling to my back. Clipboard tucked under my arm again. Smile reapplied.

New room. New faces.

Different energy.

Some had already been out exploring. A few were slightly pink from over-enthusiastic sunbathing. One man looked as though he'd already found the lunchtime beer.

And there I was again.

"Good morning, everyone…"

You repeat the same information, but you must deliver it as though it's the first time you've ever said it.

Emergency numbers.
Excursions.
Currency.
Water.
Pick-up points.

Smile.
Pause.
Invite questions.
Handle them.

Finish.

Polite applause from one enthusiastic lady in the front row. Always one.

Then straight back out into the heat.

Up the road again.

Third meeting.

By this point, I could feel the effort.

Not panic.
Not fear.

Just energy expenditure.

People assume being a rep is sunshine and sangria. And yes, those things exist. But what they don't see is the performance repetition. The emotional reset required every single time you enter a new room.

You cannot show fatigue.
You cannot rush because you've already said it twice.
You cannot let the edges fray.

Each group believes they are your only audience.

And in that moment, they are.

By the fourth meeting, because yes, there was a fourth, my throat was dry, my cheeks actually hurt from smiling, and I became acutely aware that I had been "on" since early morning.

Standing.
Walking.
Talking.
Listening.
Reassuring.

By early afternoon, when I finally sat down for the first time properly, I felt it.

Exhaustion.

Not the dramatic kind.
Not collapse-on-the-bed exhaustion.

But the deep, low-level depletion that comes from holding steady for hours.

I remember sitting on a low wall near the promenade, jacket folded beside me, tie slightly loosened, watching tourists wander past with beach towels.

They looked relaxed.
Carefree.
Holiday mode fully engaged.

And I felt… spent.

That was the moment it dawned on me.

Being a rep overseas isn't just about solving problems.

It's about sustaining presence.

You are visible all the time.
Approachable all the time.
Measured all the time.

You walk between hotels in the heat while guests wander slowly in flip-flops. You repeat the same explanations while they sip sangria. You absorb anxieties they barely admit to themselves.

And then you do it again the next day.

And the next.

And the next.

By the time I finally relaxed that afternoon, I had walked miles, spoken for hours, and answered questions I hadn't even known I'd be asked.

I remember thinking, quietly but honestly:

This is harder than it looks.

Much harder.

And strangely…

I loved it.

I didn't go straight back to the hotel.

Instead, halfway along the promenade, just near the Santa Lucia, I stopped.

There was a small bar with tables set outside under wide cream umbrellas, their fabric gently shifting in the warm breeze. The kind of place you might walk past a dozen times without noticing properly. That afternoon, it felt like salvation.

I chose a table facing the bay.

Not tucked away.

Not hidden.

Right out front.

I ordered lunch without overthinking it. Spit-roast chicken, carved straight from the turning rack inside. A simple salad. A portion of fries. And a large, ice-cold Coca-Cola.

When the drink arrived, beads of condensation clung to the outside of the glass, tiny droplets gathering and rolling slowly down onto the coaster. I wrapped my hand around it and felt the chill bite gently into my palm.

The first swallow was glorious.

Cold.

Sharp.

Alive.

It cut straight through the dryness in my throat and seemed to settle somewhere deep in my chest. I hadn't realised quite how thirsty I'd been.

I leaned back in my chair and let the noise of the resort drift around me.

Cutlery clinking.

Spanish voices behind the bar.

The low hum of conversation from nearby tables.

The faint rhythmic hush of the sea beyond the promenade.

My food arrived, golden chicken skin glistening, fries lightly salted, salad bright and simple. Nothing extraordinary.

And yet it felt like a feast.

I sat there in my uniform, tie loosened just enough, and looked out across Palma Nova bay.

The beach curved perfectly.

The water caught the sunlight like scattered diamonds.

Tourists wandered lazily with beach towels slung over shoulders.

And I felt it.

That quiet, almost dangerous thought.

I rule the world.

Not in arrogance.

Not in ego.

But in sheer disbelief.

Here I was, a lad from Whitstable, Kent, sitting under a Mediterranean sun, working overseas, trusted with responsibility, eating lunch by the sea as though this was entirely normal.

Back home in the UK, I imagined grey skies pressing low over London. Commuters under cloud cover. Damp pavements. People hurrying between tube stations and offices.

And here I was.

Warm.

Tired.

Satisfied.

Happy.

"This is the life," I remember thinking.

Not flashy.

Not extravagant.

Just… free.

For a few minutes, I allowed myself to simply exist in it.

No clipboard.

No questions.

No performance.

Just sunshine, cold cola, and the steady rhythm of an island that was beginning to feel like mine.

I had barely taken another mouthful of chicken when I heard a voice call across the road.

"Wesley!"

I looked up instinctively.

Across the promenade, just beyond the line of slow-moving tourists, I saw them.

Stephanie and Alison.

They had clearly just finished their own rounds and were walking toward the crossing, laughing about something, heads slightly tilted toward one another.

I paused mid-bite and watched them approach.

Stephanie spotted me first. Of course she did. She always seemed to scan a room, or in this case an entire stretch of promenade, like she owned it. Her curly blonde hair caught the sunlight, bouncing slightly as she walked. Even from a distance, those striking blue eyes were unmistakable. She had that effortless confidence about her, shoulders back, hips loose, movement unforced. She didn't try to be noticed.

She simply was.

Alison walked beside her, different energy entirely. Short dark hair cut neatly into that tidy bob she wore so well. Softer features. Kinder eyes. Where Stephanie's presence filled space, Alison's steadied it. She had a way of walking that felt grounded, deliberate, thoughtful, as though she was taking everything in rather than projecting outward.

They both wore their uniforms slightly differently too.

Stephanie's blazer sleeves were rolled just enough to suggest rebellion without breaking rules. Alison's shirt was buttoned properly, though her top button had long surrendered to the heat. Both had that faint sun-kissed glow already settling into their skin, early-season colour that hinted at what summer would bring.

As they crossed the road toward me, the afternoon light wrapped around them, and for a brief second, I had the surreal thought that this couldn't possibly be work.

Two attractive colleagues, Mediterranean sunshine, laughter drifting through warm air, and me sitting there in uniform under an umbrella with a cold drink.

Stephanie shaded her eyes dramatically as she approached.

"Well, look at you," she called out. "Living like a king."

Alison smiled as she reached the table, glancing at my plate.

"Spit roast chicken? Very sophisticated, Wesley."

I leaned back in my chair, trying to look nonchalant.

"Hard morning's work," I said. "Four meetings. I felt I'd earned it."

Stephanie pulled out a chair without asking and dropped into it with theatrical exhaustion.

"Oh, he's one of us now," she said to Alison. "Listen to him. Four meetings and he's rewarding himself."

Alison laughed softly as she sat down.

To anyone watching, we must have looked like carefree holidaymakers.

Only we knew that beneath the laughter was the steady hum of responsibility waiting to resume at any moment.

But for now, just for now, we were three young reps in the sun, stealing a small pocket of peace between performances.

And it felt perfect.

Stephanie didn't hesitate.

"Two Coca-Colas," she said to the waiter before Alison had even opened her mouth. "Large. With ice."

Alison laughed softly. "You didn't even ask me."

"You were going to say yes," Stephanie replied confidently.

Within moments, two tall glasses arrived, condensation already forming on the outside just like mine. Alison wrapped her fingers around hers and took a slow sip, closing her eyes briefly as the cold hit.

"Oh, that's good," she said.

Stephanie leaned back in her chair and stretched slightly, sunlight catching in her blonde curls.

"I've got a busy afternoon," she said, glancing at her watch. "Got to check the excursion sheets at the Magaluf units, chase up a coach time change, and then I've got two welcome boards to update before evening duties."

She rolled her shoulders dramatically.

"Glamorous life."

Alison looked at me over the rim of her glass.

"I'm done for now," she said. "My evening duty doesn't start until six."

There was a small pause.

She placed her glass down carefully and met my eyes properly.

"Do you fancy hanging out this afternoon? Before we start again?"

It caught me completely off guard.

Not because I didn't want to.

But because it felt… direct.

For a split second, I was aware of Stephanie watching us.

Then Stephanie gave the slightest wink, barely perceptible, but unmistakable, in Alison's direction.

Ah.

So this had already been discussed.

I tried to appear calm.

"Yeah," I said, keeping my voice level. "That sounds good."

Inside, however, something had shifted.

As Alison smiled, not broadly, just warmly, I felt a subtle but undeniable stir of awareness in my body. She was naturally beautiful. Not showy. Not theatrical like Stephanie. Just quietly, confidently attractive.

Her short dark hair framed her face neatly. Her skin carried that soft early-season glow. There was maturity in her expression, experience, something grounded and steady.

She was older than me. At least five years, maybe more.

And strangely, that made it more of a challenge.

Not intimidating exactly.

But interesting.

There's something about being the younger man in that dynamic that awakens a certain alertness. A desire not to appear naive. Not to look like the new boy.

I suddenly became very conscious of my posture. Of how I was sitting. Of whether I looked composed or like a lad who'd just discovered sangria at breakfast meetings.

Stephanie stood up first.

"Well, lovebirds," she said lightly, brushing imaginary crumbs from the table. "I'll leave you to it. Don't do anything I wouldn't do."

"That narrows it down considerably," I replied.

She laughed and gave Alison a quick look that said far more than words.

Then she walked off down the promenade, sunlight trailing behind her.

For a moment, it was just Alison and me.

The hum of the resort carried on around us, clinking glasses, distant laughter, the steady hush of the sea, but the energy at the table had changed.

Not dramatic.

Just… charged.

I took another sip of my cola, buying myself a second to settle.

"So," I said. "What did you have in mind?"

And just like that, the afternoon began to unfold into something far more interesting than I'd expected when I first sat down with a plate of chicken and fries.

Alison leaned forward slightly, resting her forearms on the table.

"Well…" she said, drawing the word out just enough to make me nervous, "Stephanie did say we can use our room this afternoon."

I blinked.

"Oh?"

She tilted her head, studying my reaction far too closely for comfort.

"So, I thought," she continued, lowering her voice just a fraction, "you might like to spend the afternoon in bed with me, Wesley."

For a full second, I stopped breathing.

I felt the heat rise instantly from my collar upwards. There was no dignified way to disguise it. I must have turned the colour of a post box.

"In… in bed?" I repeated, eloquent as ever.

My mind performed a violent leap backwards in time, Sir William Nottidge School, Whitstable. Awkward teenage dates. Holding hands near the harbour. The terrifying business of trying to kiss someone properly without knocking teeth.

And here I was.

Mediterranean sunshine.
Uniform slightly creased.

A grown woman, older than me, experienced, confident, calmly suggesting an afternoon in bed as though it were a perfectly reasonable itinerary item between lunch and evening duty.

This was not Whitstable.

This was not school.

This was not sitting nervously in a cinema sharing a bag of Revels.

This was a different world entirely.

I swallowed.

Alison watched my face with what can only be described as wicked satisfaction.

Then she burst out laughing.

"Oh, Wesley," she said, shaking her head. "I am just teasing you."

I exhaled. Possibly for the first time in ten seconds.

"Or am I…" she added lightly, eyes dancing.

My heart did an unnecessary somersault.

"No, seriously," she continued, still smiling. "I am. Although Stephanie did say the room is free."

She let that hang in the air just long enough to keep me unsettled.

"I was thinking," she went on more gently, "we could spend some time on the beach. Maybe hire a pedalo and go out on the water."

She nudged my glass lightly.

"I know you surf. I figured you'd just enjoy being near the sea."

The shift in tone was subtle but important.

Less teasing.
More thoughtful.

And that, oddly, unsettled me more than the original suggestion.

She had noticed.

Not just the rep version of me.
Not the uniform.
Not the clipboard.

The surfer.
The waterman from Whitstable.

I cleared my throat, trying to regain some composure.

"A pedalo," I said, as if I had been considering nothing else all along. "Yes. That sounds… sensible."

She smiled, satisfied.

"Don't worry," she said lightly. "I won't corrupt you entirely on your first week, but maybe in the second or third."

There it was again. That slight challenge in her tone. That knowing confidence.

And I realised something quietly in that moment.

She wasn't just teasing.

She was testing.

Seeing whether the new boy could keep up.

I stood up, trying to look steady, composed, entirely in control of my faculties.

"Right then," I said. "Beach it is."

Inside, however, I was acutely aware of two things:

One, this was a long way from teenage dating in Kent. And two, I was very much looking forward to whatever happened next.

Alison smiled, not triumphantly, not boldly, just warmly. There was something in her eyes that suggested she knew exactly how unsettled she had made me.

We left the table together, the afternoon sun still high, the Mediterranean shimmering just beyond the promenade.

For a moment, I glanced back at the umbrella, the empty glasses, the half-finished plate.

An hour earlier, I had been exhausted, questioning how demanding this job could be.

Now the day had taken on a very different energy.

This was a long way from Whitstable.

A long way from awkward teenage dates on the beach. A long way from anything predictable. The sea lay ahead of us. The rest of the afternoon unwritten.

And for the first time since arriving on the island, I felt not just like a rep. But like a young man stepping properly into his life.

Whatever happened next, it felt like something had shifted, and I had no intention of stepping backwards.

Chapter Six

As an overseas representative, selling excursions wasn't optional. It was essential.

For a start, the base salary was hardly going to fund a Mediterranean empire. Commission on trips helped top up what was, in truth, a fairly poor wage. You learned very quickly that enthusiasm translated into extra pesetas.

But it wasn't just about money.

Excursions did two important things. They brought income into the local economy, coach drivers, guides, restaurants, attraction staff, and they transformed a simple beach holiday into something memorable. A guest who lay on a sunbed all week might go home with a tan. A guest who explored the island went home with stories.

That mattered.

We were encouraged, politely but firmly, to sell and sell we did.

Every welcome meeting ended with a neatly arranged display of leaflets. Glossy photos of smiling families, underground caves, dolphins mid-leap, dramatic cliffs and cathedrals. You learned the script quickly.

"Limited spaces."
"Highly recommended."
"Books up fast in peak season."

Some reps relished it. The hard sell. The persuasive nudge. The theatrical flourish.

I was never particularly drawn to pushing Pirates Adventure or Marineland and Aquariums. They had their audience, of course.

Families loved them. Children left sticky-fingered and wide-eyed. But I never quite felt the spark talking about choreographed sword fights or dolphin shows. It just was not my thing. I know it sounds like a strange thing to admit, but it's true.

My enjoyment came elsewhere.

Palma City and the Cathedral.

The Drach Caves and Majorca Pearls.

There was something about those that felt more authentic. Palma, with its cathedral rising above the harbour, narrow streets unfolding into quiet squares, café culture humming in shaded corners. The Drach Caves, vast underground chambers where light danced across still water and classical music echoed through stone formed over millennia. The pearl factory, a little theatrical perhaps, but still a window into the island's craft and trade.

When I spoke about those trips, I didn't feel like I was selling.

I felt like I was sharing.

And guests sensed that difference.

You can't fake belief. Not convincingly. If I was animated describing Palma's old town or the cool hush of the caves, it wasn't because I'd memorised the brochure. It was because I genuinely thought they'd regret not going.

Of course, the reality of running excursions was less romantic.

It meant early mornings.
Coach manifests.

Counting heads.
Chasing latecomers.

Calming the mildly sunburnt.
Locating the missing.

Selling the dream was one thing. Delivering it was another entirely. Sometimes, even an odd romance would appear on a trip as well.

As Manuel pulled the coach up along the promenade at the agreed collection point, the engine idling with that familiar low diesel hum, I grabbed my clipboard and hopped on board.

"Hola, Manuel," I said, trying to sound like this was my natural habitat.

He nodded, as ever, steady and unflustered.

We were off to make collections around the hotels and apartment blocks in the area before heading toward Palma City and Valldemossa. A full-day experience. And if I'm honest, I was genuinely looking forward to it.

This wasn't Pirates Adventure.

This wasn't dolphins performing on cue.

This was the capital. The cathedral. The history.

The chance to explore Palma's Gothic Cathedral rising dramatically above the harbour, to wander through the narrow streets of the Old Town where the air seemed to hold centuries of conversation, and then Valldemossa, perched in the hills, stone buildings glowing in the sun, famous for its Royal Carthusian Monastery and the quiet legacy of Chopin and George Sand.

It felt cultured and almost noble.

This would be my first proper Palma excursion. I had already done a couple of the less glamorous trips, useful, profitable, perfectly fine, but this one felt different. I had been quietly hoping for the island tour, the Palma experience, or even the caves, rather than Marineland.

And now I had it.

As we pulled up at the first hotel, I stepped down from the coach with what I hoped was professional confidence.

"Palma and Valldemossa?" I called out, scanning the small crowd of guests gathering near the reception.

Hands went up. Sunhats adjusted. Cameras already hanging around necks.

"Right then," I smiled. "If you could have your tickets ready, we'll get you on board."

The first few collections went smoothly enough. Names ticked off. Seats filled. The usual light confusion over whether someone had booked for Tuesday or Thursday.

Then, at the third stop, it began.

"We booked for two," a lady insisted, clutching her handbag as though it contained state secrets.

"Yes, Mrs Thompson," I replied calmly, checking the manifest. "I have you and Mr Thompson."

"Well, he's just gone back to the room to get his camera."

I glanced at my watch.

"Do you know how long he'll be?"

"Oh, not long."

Which in holiday language could mean anything from thirty seconds to ten minutes and a full wardrobe change.

The coach behind me idled. Manuel glanced in the mirror. The rest of the guests were beginning to settle into their seats, unaware that the entire itinerary hinged on one man locating a camera.

I smiled politely.

"I'll give him two minutes," I said.

In rep life, two minutes rarely means two minutes.

Sure enough, five passed.

Just as I was contemplating sending Mrs Thompson up to retrieve her wandering photographer, he appeared, jogging lightly, camera triumphantly raised like a trophy.

"Got it!" he called.

We boarded. Doors closed. Crisis averted.

And we were finally on our way.

As the coach rolled out along the coast road toward Palma, the morning sun climbing steadily higher, I stood at the front with the microphone in hand.

There's a particular moment on excursions when you stop being the rep collecting bodies and become the guide shaping the day.

"Ladies and gentlemen," I began, steadier now than I had been during my first welcome meeting, "Palma City and Valldemossa…"

And as the coastline slipped past the window and the cathedral's silhouette slowly emerged in the distance, I felt that same quiet surge of excitement I'd had when I first glimpsed the island from the aircraft window.

Only this time, I wasn't arriving.

I was leading.

And that, I realised, was an entirely different thrill.

We had only just settled into the steady rhythm of the road when it happened.

There was no warning.

Just a sudden, explosive bang that tore through the side of the coach, followed by a violent shudder beneath our feet. The steering jerked sharply, and I felt the entire vehicle lurch sideways as Manuel fought the wheel.

For a split second, time seemed to stretch.

The coach swerved toward the barrier. Metal scraped against metal with a grinding shriek that made my teeth clench. Somewhere toward the back, a woman screamed. A bag fell from an overhead rack. Someone shouted, "What's happening?"

Then, almost as quickly, we were slowing.

Manuel corrected the wheel with a calmness that, in hindsight, was extraordinary. The coach scraped along the guard rail for what felt like far too long, before he steered us safely onto the side of the road.

Silence followed.

Not complete silence, engines ticking, nervous breathing, a child whimpering somewhere near the rear, but the kind of stunned quiet that settles after something almost goes very wrong.

Manuel wiped his brow with the back of his hand and raised his eyebrows at me.

"Eso fue cerca," he said under his breath.

That was close.

He reached for the door lever and hopped down onto the roadside without drama.

I picked up the microphone, aware that every pair of eyes was now on me.

"Ladies and gentlemen," I said as evenly as I could manage, though my pulse was still hammering in my ears, "please remain seated and calm. I'm just going to step outside and see what's happened. We'll update you in a few minutes."

The important thing in moments like that is tone.

Not too cheerful.
Not alarmed.
Just steady.

I stepped down from the coach and walked around to the nearside.

The smell hit me first, hot rubber and faint metal. Then I saw it.

The front tyre had completely blown.

Not a slow puncture. Not a gentle deflation.

It had exploded.

Shredded rubber hung loosely from the wheel arch, and the rim bore the scuffed marks of where we had clipped the guard rail. At the speed we had been travelling, it could have been far worse. Much worse.

I looked back at the stretch of road we had just travelled. A curve. A drop beyond the barrier.

My stomach tightened slightly at the thought of what might have happened if Manuel had panicked.

But he hadn't.

That is something I have always found, not only in Mallorca but across mainland Spain as well: Spanish coach drivers are to be respected. Deeply respected. They grow up navigating narrow mountain passes, tight village corners, unpredictable traffic, roads that would make most British drivers hesitate.

They don't flap.

They react.

Manuel had reacted.

He crouched beside the damaged tyre, examining it with the quiet focus of someone who had seen worse in his time. No theatrics. No raised voice. Just calm assessment.

I stood there for a moment, the sun suddenly feeling hotter than before, the reality of what had almost occurred settling gently but firmly into my mind.

Inside that coach were thirty-odd guests who had entrusted their day, and, in a sense, their safety, to us.

And for the first time that morning, the job felt heavier.

Not dramatic.

Just real.

I took a slow breath, straightened my shirt instinctively, and turned back toward the coach doors.

Time to go and steady the room again.

After stepping back onto the coach and explaining clearly what had happened, I reassured the guests that we were safe and that I would update them shortly. There was a murmur of conversation, but no panic. Just that slightly heightened awareness that follows an unexpected jolt.

"I'll be back with more information in a few minutes," I said, placing the microphone back in its holder.

I stepped down again to find Manuel standing beside the wheel, arms raised slightly in frustration.

He had tried the radio.

But we were in an awkward dip in the road, surrounded by low hills, and the signal simply wasn't getting through cleanly to the depot. The radio crackled uselessly in reply.

And of course, in those days, there were no mobile phones tucked into pockets to rescue us.

Communication meant wires, radio waves, and hope.

As we stood there considering our options, I noticed movement on the opposite side of the road. A coach approaching from the direction of Palma.

Blue and white livery.

Ours.

Without really thinking, I jogged across the road and began waving both arms in what I hoped looked authoritative rather than desperate.

The coach slowed. Then stopped.

As the doors opened, I recognised it immediately, an airport transfer run. And there, halfway down the aisle, was Stephanie, grinning broadly and waving as though this were all part of some elaborate plan.

She stepped down onto the roadside.

"What on earth have you done?" she laughed.

"Blown tyre," I replied. "And a bit of guard rail."

At the same time, her driver, Esteban, had climbed down and joined Manuel. The two of them stood beside the damaged wheel, hands on hips, nodding and gesturing in animated

Spanish. Looking back now, it must have been a slightly comical tableau, two Spanish drivers studying a ruined tyre while two young British reps hovered nearby trying to look competent.

At the time, however, it was entirely serious.

I asked Stephanie if she could stop at her first drop-off point and telephone the coach depot with Esteban. We needed a replacement coach sent out as soon as possible, or at the very least roadside assistance to repair the tyre so the excursion could continue.

She nodded immediately.

"Of course," she said. "We'll sort it."

There was no drama. No fuss. Just practical cooperation.

I thanked her, and she gave me a quick look, part concern, part amusement, before climbing back aboard her coach.

As they pulled away, I crossed back to my stranded passengers.

I stepped up inside and explained the situation again clearly. Replacement coach being arranged. No danger. Just a delay.

And this is where something rather lovely happened.

An older gentleman sitting near the front chuckled and said loudly enough for several rows to hear, "Well, this is an adventure. Would've paid extra for this bit of excitement!"

Laughter rippled through the coach.

His wife shook her head affectionately beside him.

It was such a very British response to a near mishap, deflect tension with humour.

And then, right on cue, someone from further back called out:

"Anywhere we can grab a cup of tea while we're waiting?"

More laughter.

It broke the tension entirely.

I stepped back down onto the road and glanced along the bend. Just a short walk ahead, perhaps three or four hundred yards, I could see a small café-bar perched beside the roadside.

I spoke quietly with Manuel.

We agreed the coach was stable and safely positioned. No immediate danger. Traffic was light.

So, I climbed back up the steps and addressed the group.

"There's a café just down the road," I said. "Rather than sitting here, I suggest we take a short walk and wait there. As soon as the replacement coach arrives, we'll collect you and continue."

There were nods of approval.

Within minutes, I had thirty-odd guests walking in a loose line along the roadside toward tea and shade. Cameras out again. Conversations resuming. Crisis already turning into anecdote.

Before following them, I turned back to Manuel.

"Use the café phone as well," I said. "Just in case."

Redundancy. Always redundancy.

He nodded.

And so there we were, an entire Palma and Valldemossa excursion temporarily relocated to a roadside café because of a blown tyre.

Not glamorous.

Not in the brochure.

But absolutely part of being an overseas rep.

And strangely, as I walked behind the group toward the café, making sure no one lagged too far behind, I felt something steady settle inside me again.

This was the real job.

Not just selling the dream.

Managing it when it wobbled.

The replacement coach arrived just over an hour later.

Long enough for two rounds of coffee and tea, several photographs beside the roadside, and a surprisingly pleasant conversation with the café owner who seemed entirely unbothered by the sudden arrival of thirty British tourists and happy to have helped.

When the fresh coach finally appeared around the bend, there was a small ripple of applause from our group. It wasn't theatrical, just relieved and appreciative.

Manuel had already arranged the transfer of bags, belongings and paperwork, and within minutes we were boarding again, tickets rechecked, heads counted carefully this time with perhaps a little more attention than before.

I stood at the front once everyone was seated, microphone in hand once more.

"Right," I said, smiling, "second attempt."

There were a few chuckles.

Before we pulled away, I had stepped into the café to use the telephone and called the office. I asked them to inform all the return hotels that we would be arriving later than scheduled and that some guests might miss the standard dinner sitting. I requested that plates be kept aside where necessary.

It was a small detail, but an important one.

The last thing anyone needed after an unexpected roadside delay was to arrive back tired and hungry only to be told the kitchen had closed.

When we were properly on the move again, the cathedral slowly growing larger on the horizon, I addressed the group.

"I've contacted the office," I explained. "All your hotels are aware we'll be returning later than planned. Dinner will be held for those who need it."

There were nods of appreciation.

"And listen," I added lightly, "we've already had a proper adventure this morning. Not many tourists get to experience an authentic roadside café in Mallorca on their way to Palma."

That drew laughter.

"We'll still enjoy the full excursion," I continued. "The cathedral isn't going anywhere, Valldemossa hasn't moved, and we've gained a story to tell."

The mood on the coach had shifted entirely now.

What could have turned sour had instead become part of the day's narrative. People were chatting more freely. The older gentleman at the front was already retelling the tyre story as though it had been a planned feature.

As we curved into Palma and the great Gothic cathedral rose into full view against the blue sky, I felt something settle quietly inside me.

An hour lost.
A potential disaster avoided.
Thirty guests calm and still willing to enjoy the day.

That wasn't luck.

That was management.

And as we rolled toward the city centre, I realised that being a rep wasn't about preventing every problem.

It was about how you handled them when they arrived.

As the coach eased into Palma and the traffic slowed to a gentle crawl, the cathedral revealed itself properly for the first time.

Even now, decades later, I can still picture that moment.

La Seu.

Rising from the edge of the harbour like something carved from sunlight and sandstone. Its Gothic spires pierced the blue sky with quiet authority, impossibly tall, impossibly intricate.

The sea shimmered just beyond it, and the whole scene felt almost staged, as if someone had arranged it purely for dramatic effect.

I stood at the front of the coach and gestured toward it.

"Ladies and gentlemen," I said, unable to hide my own admiration, "welcome to Palma."

There were audible murmurs.

A few cameras clicked instinctively.

When we disembarked, the warmth wrapped around us fully. Not oppressive, just generous. The kind of Mediterranean warmth that settles into your shoulders and makes you breathe a little more slowly.

We were met by a local guide in the square, a slender Mallorcan woman in her forties with sharp features, kind eyes, and the calm confidence of someone who knew every stone of the city. Her English was excellent, lightly accented, and she carried a small folder tucked neatly under her arm.

"Bienvenidos a Palma," she began, smiling at the group. "Today we walk through history."

And that is exactly what it felt like.

We moved slowly through the narrow streets of the Old Town, the sound of our footsteps echoing gently off ancient walls. The air carried a mixture of warm stone, coffee drifting from nearby cafés, and something faintly floral from hidden courtyards.

The streets were not wide or grand in the way London might be.

They were intimate.

Balconies leaned overhead. Wooden shutters stood half-open. Small plaques marked buildings older than any structure most of our guests had ever stood inside back home.

Our guide spoke of kings and bishops, of Moorish influence and Christian reconquest, of centuries layered quietly one upon another. She pointed out architectural details most of us would

have walked past without noticing, carved lintels, hidden coats of arms, the subtle curve of an arch that revealed an older civilisation beneath.

The group slowed naturally.

This was no longer a beach crowd.

They were listening.

Inside the cathedral, the scale swallowed us whole. Shafts of coloured light filtered through stained glass, casting shifting pools of red and blue across the stone floor. The ceiling seemed impossibly high, as though gravity had been politely suspended for aesthetic reasons.

One of the more boisterous gentlemen from earlier removed his hat instinctively.

Even the children were quiet.

I watched the guests rather than the architecture for a moment.

Faces tilted upward.
Eyes wide.
Voices lowered.

The older couple who had joked about the tyre stood hand in hand near a column, simply looking.

That is what I loved about this excursion.

It changed people's posture.

It pulled them out of sunbeds and into centuries.

As we moved back out into the daylight and into the small squares dotted with cafés and orange trees, something had shifted in the group. Conversations were animated again, but now they carried phrases like "can you believe how old that was?" and "imagine building that without machinery."

There is a particular joy in watching guests discover something they hadn't expected.

Palma wasn't loud.
It wasn't flashy.
It didn't need to be.

It was confident in its history.

And as we wandered toward the shaded square where we would later regroup before heading up to Valldemossa, I felt quietly vindicated.

This was why I preferred selling Palma.

Not because it paid more.
Not because it sounded impressive in a brochure.

But because it gave people something lasting.

A tan fades.
A photograph gathers dust.

But standing inside a Gothic cathedral for the first time, hearing your footsteps echo in a space built centuries before your country industrialised, that stays with you.

I caught the eye of the older gentleman from the front row.

"Well worth the blown tyre," he said, grinning.

I smiled.

"Yes," I replied. "I think so."

And in that moment, walking through Palma with a group who had started the morning skidding along a guard rail and were now marvelling at medieval architecture, I understood something more deeply about this job.

It wasn't just about logistics.

It was about transformation.

By the time we left Valldemossa, the afternoon light had softened into that gentle Mallorcan glow that seems to round the edges of everything it touches.

The village had been exactly what I had hoped it would be for the guests. Stone houses stacked neatly along narrow lanes. Terracotta pots bursting with colour. The monastery cool and still inside, its cloisters offering shade from the sun. We had even found a quiet patch of ground for a simple picnic lunch, bread, olives, cheese, fruit, and, inevitably, another jug of sangria, which seemed to follow British tourists wherever they travelled.

There is something about eating outdoors after a long day that deepens conversation. People relax differently. Stories are shared more freely. The tyre incident had already become folklore by then, retold with increasing exaggeration and laughter.

As we made our way back down toward Palma and eventually along the coast road toward the resorts, the coach was noticeably quieter.

Sun and culture combined is a powerful sedative.

Heads leaned against windows. Conversations faded. A gentle hum replaced the earlier chatter. I stood at the front for a while,

then eventually sat down beside Manuel, both of us content in the silence.

When we began dropping guests back at their hotels, there were handshakes. "Thank you". A few comments about what a "memorable" day it had been.

And then, just like that, they were gone.

The coach emptied.
The clipboard closed.
The microphone silent.

By the time I returned to the Santa Lucia, I felt it fully.

Exhaustion.

Not just physical tiredness, though my legs certainly knew how many steps we had walked, but mental depletion. The kind that comes from holding responsibility all day, from watching for problems that might not even materialise, from remaining steady when something could easily have spiralled.

I made my way to the restaurant and found a table near the corner.

The head waiter spotted me immediately.

"Señor Wesley," he said warmly, placing a hand briefly over his heart before setting down a glass of chilled rosé without even asking. The condensation on the glass caught the light of the afternoon – perfection!

I smiled in gratitude.

The first sip was soft and cooling, the faint fruitiness settling me in a way water simply couldn't.

My plate arrived soon after, simple hotel fare, but after a long day it might as well have been five-starred.

I had barely taken a second mouthful when I heard familiar voices approaching.

Stephanie and Alison appeared at the table.

Not carrying plates.
Not dressed for evening duty, just casual clothes.

Just… arriving.

"Heard what a day you had," Alison said as she pulled out a chair.

Stephanie leaned one hip against the table before sitting down. "Nearly lost a coach and still delivered the cultural tour of the season."

I shook my head, half-smiling.

"It wasn't quite like that."

"Oh, it was," Stephanie insisted. "I've already overheard two of your guests in the bar telling someone they'd had the best day of their holiday."

Alison nodded. "Really well organised. And calm, from what I gather."

Stephanie glanced at me. "Not sure I'd have been that steady with a blown tyre and a guard rail involved."

I took another sip of wine.

"Well," I said quietly, "I'm very tired."

That earned a softer look from Alison.

"And mentally drained as well," I added. "If I'm honest… probably a little shocked too."

They both fell quiet.

"We could have had a far more severe accident," I continued, looking down briefly at the tablecloth before meeting their eyes again. "If it hadn't been for Manuel's driving, it could have been very different."

Stephanie nodded seriously now.

"He's good," she said.

"He's exceptional," I replied. "We were lucky."

There was a pause, not awkward, just reflective.

The adrenaline had long faded, and what remained was the understanding of how close things can sometimes come to shifting entirely.

Alison reached across the table briefly and squeezed my hand. Not dramatic. Not performative. Just present.

"You handled it," she said quietly.

And in that moment, I realised something else about the job.

It wasn't just about being calm for guests.

It was about carrying the weight afterward too.

I leaned back slightly, glass in hand, the restaurant gently humming around us, and allowed myself to feel both things at once.

Exhausted.

And quietly proud.

Alison left her hand resting lightly on mine.

She didn't remove it.

Just kept it there, her thumb gently pressing against my skin, as though steadying me without making a show of it.

Stephanie saw it.

There was the faintest flicker in her expression, not jealousy exactly, just awareness, and she stood up with theatrical timing.

"Well," she said lightly, "I'll leave you two to debrief properly. I've got paperwork to pretend to finish."

She gave Alison a look. A knowing one.

Then she was gone.

The restaurant noise continued around us, but at our table something quieter had settled.

Alison didn't move her hand.

She studied me for a moment.

"You're still in shock," she said gently.

"I'm fine," I replied automatically.

She shook her head slightly.

"You're not shaking," she said, "but it's there. You're replaying it."

She was right.

I wasn't panicked. I wasn't distressed. But somewhere in the back of my mind, the image of the guard rail and the curve in the road kept flashing briefly.

The responsibility of it all.

Thirty guests.
One split second.
One driver's reaction.

"We carry a lot, don't we?" I said quietly.

She squeezed my hand again.

"Yes," she replied. "We do."

She took a slow breath and then, with that same steady tone, said, "Let's go for a drink later. When you've finished here."

I looked up.

"I'll come up while you shower and change," she continued,

matter of factly. "And then we can relax properly this evening. If you'd like that."

There was no performance in her voice now.

Just warmth.

"I'd like that," I said.

We went upstairs together, not touching this time, but close enough that our shoulders brushed once in the corridor.

I unlocked my door and let her in.

She moved naturally toward the balcony, opening the doors slightly to let the evening air drift inside.

"I'll be quick," I said, suddenly very aware of the day still clinging to me, heat, dust, adrenaline.

In the bathroom, as the water ran over my shoulders, I let the tension finally drain. The noise of the shower muted everything else. For a few minutes, I stood there, eyes closed, replaying the day, the bang, the swerve, the laughter in the café, the cathedral light.

When I stepped out and dressed, I reached automatically for Kouros, a scent that, at the time, felt like adulthood in a bottle.

When I opened the bathroom door, she was standing on the balcony.

Moonlight lay softly across the bay, the water dark now but shimmering faintly where it caught the light. The promenade below had quietened, the occasional voice drifting upward from passing tourists.

Alison had poured herself a glass of rosé from the bottle I'd left in the room. She held it loosely in one hand, her silhouette framed against the night.

She turned as she heard me.

For a moment, she simply looked at me.

The moonlight caught the curve of her cheek, the line of her hair. She looked different in the evening, softer, less rep, more woman.

She extended her free hand toward me.

"Come here," she said quietly.

I stepped beside her.

"Wesley," she said, gazing out across the water, "we are so lucky, don't you think?"

I followed her eyes.

"Just look at this," she continued. "We get to live here. Work here. See this every day. Most people only dream about it."

She was right.

"Yes," I said softly. "We are lucky."

She turned toward me.

And before my mind had fully processed what was happening, her arms had wrapped around me.
It wasn't hesitant.

It wasn't tentative.

Her lips found mine with a confidence that stole whatever breath I had left.

The kiss was warm, certain, and utterly unlike anything I had known back in Kent. This wasn't schoolyard nervousness. This was a woman who understood exactly what she wanted.

When she pulled away, she didn't step back.

She kept her hands resting against my chest.

"Wesley," she said, voice low but steady, "let's stay here tonight. Just enjoy this. I'm not going back next door."

She held my gaze.

"Let's have our moment."

There was a pause.

Not long.

Just long enough for me to realise how completely different this was from anything I had experienced before.

"Is that okay?" she asked gently.

I looked at her, at the calm certainty in her expression, at the moonlit bay behind her, at the strange, beautiful life I had stepped into.

"Yes," I said simply.

And I meant it.

I was blown away.

Chapter Seven

If the previous day had taught me anything, it was that the life of an overseas representative was never quite as smooth as the brochures suggested.

For every postcard moment, cathedral light streaming through ancient windows, sangria shared in quiet villages, or moonlit conversations on balconies, there was always something else waiting quietly around the corner.

Problems.

They arrived in many forms.

Lost passports.

Sunburn that turned to illness.

Arguments between couples who had clearly brought more baggage than their suitcases contained. Guests who drank too much under the generous Mediterranean sun and forgot entirely how to behave in public.

And then there were the hotel issues.

Rooms not as expected. Air conditioning that refused to cooperate. Noise complaints. Missing luggage.

Misunderstandings that somehow landed squarely on the rep's shoulders to resolve.

What no training manual ever fully explained was this:

As a rep, you absorb everything.

The guests' frustrations.

The hotel's explanations.

The tour operator's expectations.

You stand in the middle and quietly take the pressure from all sides.

Sometimes the problems were small.

Sometimes they were not.

And on this particular morning, as I walked along the promenade into one of the units I was responsible for in Palma Nova, clipboard tucked under my arm and already mentally preparing for the morning surgery hour, I could see immediately that something was wrong.

A woman was crying in the reception area.

She sat on one of the low sofas near the desk, clutching her handbag tightly against her chest as though it might somehow contain the solution to whatever had happened.

Her husband stood beside her, pacing in short, agitated steps, running his hands repeatedly through his thinning hair.

I paused for a moment before approaching.

You learn quickly as a rep that rushing into a situation rarely helps. First, you observe. Then you step in.

"Good morning," I said calmly. "Is everything alright?"

The husband turned toward me almost immediately.

"No," he said bluntly. "It's not."

He gestured toward his wife.

"She, that thing there, has lost her passport."

There are certain words that, as a rep, immediately trigger a quiet alarm bell.

Lost passport was one of them, and having him insult her in such a manner was another.

The words hung in the air for a moment.

"She's lost her passport."

I nodded slowly, not reacting too quickly, because experience, even the little I had gained so far, had already taught me that lost passports often weren't lost at all.

They were misplaced.

Hidden.

Tucked somewhere so carefully that nobody could remember where.

"Alright," I said calmly. "Let's start at the beginning."

The woman wiped her eyes with a tissue she had clearly already used several times that morning.

"I had it yesterday," she said. "I know I did."

Her husband folded his arms, frustration written all over his face.

"We've turned the whole room upside down," he said. "Suitcases, drawers, bags, everything."

I nodded again.

"Well," I replied gently, "let's go and have another look together."

Often, that was all it took. A fresh pair of eyes and a slower, calmer search.

We walked upstairs to their room. As they opened the door, it was immediately clear that they had not exaggerated their earlier statement.

The place looked like a small storm had passed through.

Clothes lay draped over chairs. Suitcases were open on the beds. Handbags and beach bags had been emptied across the small table.

Lost passports create a very particular kind of panic. People search quickly, not carefully.

"I promise you," the husband said as we stepped inside, "we've looked everywhere."

I smiled slightly.

"That's usually when they turn up."

I began working through the room methodically. Not rushing. Just checking places calmly.

In those days, many hotels and apartment units didn't have room safes. Instead, valuables were usually kept behind the reception desk, where guests could rent a small safety box for the week.

Sometimes it costs five pesetas. Sometimes ten.

It was hardly a fortune, but even so, some guests preferred to keep their documents in the room rather than pay the small charge.

Which meant passports often ended up in strange places.

Inside books.

Under pillows.

In jacket pockets that hadn't been worn since the flight.

I opened the wardrobe.

"Checked in here?" I asked.

"Three times," the husband replied.

Still, I moved the hanging clothes aside one by one. Jackets. Dresses. A pair of trousers.

And then I noticed something near the back.

A small dark shape was resting awkwardly against the wooden panel.

I reached in and pulled it forward.

A British passport, which in those days was large and solid dark blue or practically black, with the name handwritten on the top.

There was a moment of silence.

Then the woman gasped.

"Oh, my goodness… that's it!"

She practically rushed across the room and took it from my hand, turning it over as though confirming it hadn't somehow transformed into something else.

"How did it get there?" she said, half laughing now through the remnants of earlier tears.

I looked at the wardrobe rail.

"My guess," I said, "is it slipped out of a pocket or bag and fell behind the clothes."

The husband let out a long breath.

"Well I'll be damned."

Just minutes earlier the holiday had been over.

Now it was restored by a small blue booklet hiding quietly behind a row of shirts.

The transformation in the room was immediate.

Relief flooded in.

"Thank you," the woman said earnestly. "I don't know what we would have done."

"Well," I replied lightly, "we would have sorted it out one way or another."

Which was true.

But it would have involved a police report, embassy visits in Palma, and a good deal more paperwork than any of us would have enjoyed.

As I left the apartment and made my way back down toward reception, I allowed myself a small smile. The crisis had lasted less than thirty minutes. But for those guests, it had felt like the end of the world. And that was the second lesson of being a rep.

Problems are rarely as large as they first appear. But in the moment, to the person experiencing them, they feel enormous.

And your job is simply to stand calmly in the middle of that storm until it passes.

No sooner had the passport drama settled than the next problem appeared.

That was another thing about being a rep. Problems rarely arrived one at a time.

Later that same morning, while I was still working through my unit visits and while walking through the backstreets of Palma Nova, a couple approached me looking visibly shaken. The wife clutched her arms tightly across her chest while her husband stood beside her trying to remain calm, though it was obvious that both of them had just been through something unpleasant.

"My bag's been stolen," she said immediately.

There was no mistaking the distress in her voice.

It had happened only minutes earlier along the beachfront promenade, in broad daylight. The area was busy with tourists drifting between cafés, souvenir shops and the beach, the sort of relaxed holiday scene where people naturally drop their guard.

She explained what had happened.

Someone had approached her politely and asked the time. The voice, she said, had sounded delicate, almost soft and hesitant, and she had instinctively leaned slightly forward to look down at her watch.

In that brief moment of distraction, someone else must have moved in.

Her handbag had disappeared.

It was the sort of trick that only works when practised properly. Two people working together, one distracting, the other lifting the bag before the victim even realises what has happened.

An organised pickpocket operation.

Unfortunately, Mallorca and mainland Spain, for that matter, in the 1980's and early 1990's had always attracted this.

She was understandably in a real state.

The first thing in situations like that is to move quickly but calmly.

"Right," I said gently. "First, we need to go to the police station and file a report."

The Spanish police required an official statement before anything else could happen. Insurance companies would not even begin to process a claim without a formal police report.

So, I arranged a taxi to take her to the local police station, and I went with her, the husband quietly explaining what had been inside the bag.

A small purse.

Some cash and two credit cards with TSB and Barclays Bank.

Sunglasses.

It could have been worse.

At the station, we waited for our turn; the atmosphere inside was surprisingly calm. The officers were clearly used to this sort of thing. Mallorca had been welcoming tourists for some time, and pickpocketing complaints were unfortunately not uncommon during the summer season.

Once the statement had been taken and the paperwork completed, we stepped outside again into the warm midday sun.

The next step was to telephone their insurance company in the UK and begin the claims process. So, I arranged a Taxi back to the hotel unit. Before doing that, however, I asked the practical question that often mattered most in that moment.

"Do you still have access to money?"

The husband nodded.

"Yes," he said. "Most of it is in the hotel safe."

That was good news.

In fact, he smiled slightly despite the circumstances.

"Best fifteen pesetas I've spent in Majorca," he added.

I laughed.

The small fee that hotels charged for safety boxes behind reception suddenly seemed like a very wise investment indeed.

They were clearly experienced travellers. They understood the basics of looking after valuables abroad. Unfortunately, even experienced travellers can be undone by a clever pickpocket working a crowded promenade.

"Don't worry," I reassured them. "We'll get everything sorted.".

Guests arrive on holiday expecting sunshine and relaxation.

But sometimes what they really need is someone who knows exactly what to do when things go wrong. And that person, often, was the overseas rep.

By the time the police report had been completed, the taxi arranged, and the couple reassured that their insurance claim process was underway, the day had almost completely disappeared.

What had started as a routine set of hotel and apartment complex visits had quickly turned into something else entirely.

That, I was beginning to realise, was the nature of the job.

You could plan your day perfectly, welcome meetings, excursions, guest visits and paperwork, but the reality of being an overseas representative often meant spending the entire day solving problems instead.

Eventually I made my way back toward the Santa Lucia hotel, feeling the kind of tiredness that doesn't come from physical effort alone but from constant responsibility.

It had already been a very eventful day, and in truth I had hardly carried out any of the normal rep duties that would usually fill my morning.

Although many experienced reps would probably argue that what I had been doing all day was exactly the real work of the job.

As I walked into the hotel reception area, the receptionist immediately called me over.

"Señor Wesley," she said, gesturing toward the desk. "There is a telephone message for you. The office has asked that you call them as soon as possible."

That was never usually a good sign.

I stepped behind the reception desk and used the phone to call the local office.

After a brief exchange with the operations team, the situation became clear.

One of my guests had been taken to a nearby clinic earlier that morning after suffering what appeared to be a stroke.

His wife was with him at the hospital.

And they needed the rep.

There was no hesitation.

Within minutes, I had arranged another taxi and was heading toward the clinic.

The drive was quiet. Mallorca slipped past the window, beachgoers, cafés, the ordinary rhythm of holiday life continuing as normal, while my mind began working through what needed to happen next.

When I arrived at the clinic, I found the guest resting in a hospital bed, pale and clearly exhausted. His wife sat beside him, her face showing the strain of the morning's events.

She looked visibly relieved the moment she saw me.

"I'm so glad you're here," she said.

Medical situations were a different kind of challenge altogether.

This was no longer about missing luggage or lost documents.

Now we were dealing with health, hospitals and the reality that holidays sometimes take very unexpected turns.

The couple had originally been scheduled to return to the United Kingdom the following day. Clearly, that was no longer possible.

Which meant the next stage of the rep's job would begin. I needed to contact our UK head office, complete incident reports and begin liaising with the repatriation team who handled medical cases abroad.

Over the rest of the day, there would be phone calls, paperwork, medical updates and decisions to make about whether the guest would eventually travel home with medical assistance or remain in Mallorca longer while recovering.

Their flights would need to be changed.

Their hotel arrangements extended.

Insurance companies contacted.

Doctors consulted.

It was a process that could take days, sometimes even weeks.

As I sat beside the hospital bed speaking with the couple and reassuring them that we would help organise everything, I realised something important.

The job of an overseas rep was never really about selling excursions or organising welcome meetings.

At its heart, the job was about people. And sometimes, when things went wrong far from home, simply being there for someone was the most important part of the role.

Eventually, once everything that could be done that day had been arranged and the doctors were satisfied that the guest was stable, I stepped outside the clinic and into the warm early evening air and made my way back to the resort.

In Palma Nova, life was still alive with the gentle rhythm of holiday life. Couples walked slowly along the promenade. Families drifted between cafés and restaurants. The sea shimmered quietly under the fading light of the sun.

For the thousands of visitors enjoying their week in Mallorca, the evening meant relaxation.

For me, it felt like the end of a very long day.

I eventually made my way back toward the Santa Lucia hotel, the tiredness now settling properly into my shoulders. It had been a day filled with problems, decisions and responsibility, the kind of day that no training manual could really prepare you for.

I could hear from a bar, Dire Straits being played, "The Walk of Life", and I thought how appropriate it was, and as I walked through the reception area, I heard a familiar voice.

"Wesley!"

I turned to see Alison walking toward me from the bar area, a glass in her hand and that easy smile she seemed to carry with her wherever she went.

"You look exhausted," she said, stopping in front of me.

I laughed softly.

"That obvious?"

"Very."

She tilted her head slightly.

"I heard about the hospital situation."

News travelled quickly among reps.

I nodded.

"Yes. It's been one of those days."

She didn't say anything for a moment. Instead, she stepped forward and wrapped her arms around me in a warm, reassuring hug.

It wasn't dramatic.

It wasn't romantic.

It was simply the quiet understanding that sometimes exists between people who share the same strange job and the same strange lifestyle.

Other reps understood in ways that nobody else really could, like a hidden family code in many ways, and one that I belonged to, and now would always be part of.

When she stepped back, she held up her glass.

"Come and have a drink," she said gently. "You've earned it."

I followed her toward the bar, feeling the tension of the day slowly begin to ease.

And as we sat together looking out across the evening lights of Palma Nova, I realised something else about my new life.

For the guests, Mallorca was sunshine, sangria and carefree holidays. For us, it was something far more complicated. But somehow, that was exactly what made it unforgettable.

Chapter Eight

One of the strange things about being an overseas rep was that you were never really alone, yet at times you could feel very separate from everyone around you.

The team of reps formed a kind of travelling family. We worked together, lived near each other, shared stories, dealt with problems, and, more often than not, ended our evenings in the same bars or restaurants somewhere along the resort strip.

On the surface, it looked like a carefree life.

Sunshine, late nights, laughter and the constant hum of holidaymakers enjoying themselves. But like any small community thrown together in intense circumstances, there were layers beneath it all.

Friendships formed quickly.

So did rivalries.

There was gossip, of course. There always is when you place a group of outgoing people together in a foreign country for months at a time. Who was seeing whom, who had fallen out with whom, who had made a mistake with a guest or upset someone in the office.

News travelled quickly through the rep network.

Sometimes faster than it should have.

What I began to notice fairly early on was that I seemed to divide opinion rather sharply.

People either liked me very much or they didn't like me at all. There was very little middle ground. Later in life, I would hear the phrase "like Marmite."

At the time, I didn't have those exact words for it, but the meaning was already clear. Some of the team enjoyed my company and my slightly different outlook on things. Others clearly thought I was a little not for them or a threat.

Part of the reason, I think, was that my version of life as a rep didn't quite match the stereotype that many people expected.

A lot of reps lived for the nightlife.

Long evenings that stretched well into the early hours, moving from one bar to another, dancing, drinking and socialising with guests and other reps.

And there was nothing wrong with that. For many people, it was exactly the kind of adventure they had come abroad to experience. But increasingly, I found myself drawn in a slightly different direction.

Of course, I enjoyed a good evening out with the team from time to time. Those moments of laughter and shared stories were part of the bond that reps developed with each other.

Yet more and more often, I found myself wandering off alone.

Sometimes it would be a quiet walk along the coastline as the sun was setting.

Other times, I would catch a bus and wander through parts of the capital Palma itself, exploring its streets, cafés and small corners of the island that most tourists never see.

Mallorca, to me, was not just a resort, a party in the sunshine, it was magical.

It was a place full of culture, history and quiet beauty waiting just beyond the main strip of bars and souvenir shops.

I began to realise that my experience of being a rep was slowly becoming different from that of many others.

While some of the teams were discovering the island's nightlife, I was discovering the island itself. Neither approach was right nor wrong.

They were simply different.

And it was around this time that I also began to learn another important lesson about working overseas with a close-knit team.

Not everyone was a friend.

Some people would support you when things went wrong. Others would quietly enjoy watching you struggle. Part of growing into the job meant learning the difference.

And that lesson, like many others that summer, would arrive sooner than I expected.

I found myself at one of the informal rep gatherings that seemed to happen most weeks somewhere along the strip.

The bars in Palma Nova and Magaluf were lively late into the evening. Music spilt out onto the pavements, neon lights flickered above crowded doorways, and groups of holidaymakers drifted slowly from one place to the next in search of another drink and another story to take home with them. The resort carried that unmistakable energy that only Mediterranean holiday towns seem to produce after dark.

On this particular night, a handful of reps had gathered in one of the larger bars, with Bacardi and Cokes flowing freely. It was the sort of place that always seemed busy during all seasons, a constant mixture of holidaymakers, bar staff shouting drink orders, and the occasional familiar face passing through. Glasses clinked, laughter rose above the music, and the warm air carried the mixture of perfume, sun cream and cigarette smoke that seemed to define the nightlife of the late 1980s.

I sat with the group for a while, listening more than speaking. Some of the conversations were the usual rep stories, difficult guests, funny situations from excursions, and small disasters that had somehow been resolved by the end of the day. Anyone who had worked overseas long enough knew that these stories became the currency of rep life, each one retold with increasing humour as the evening went on.

Other conversations drifted, as they often did, into gossip.

That was another constant within the rep world. When a group of young people live and work abroad together for months at a time, stories travel quickly. Someone was always talking about someone else, who had been late for a transfer, who had upset the office, who had been seen leaving a bar with a rep from another company. It was rarely malicious, but it was rarely particularly kind either.

At one point, I stood up from the table and made my way to the bar to order another drink. As I waited, leaning slightly against the counter and watching the barman working his way through the evening rush, I heard two voices behind me.

They belonged to a pair of reps who had joined our table earlier in the night. One of them lowered his voice slightly, though not quite enough to avoid being overheard.

"That Wesley," he said.

There was a short pause before the other replied.

"What about him?"

"I can't quite work him out," the first voice said. "Bit strange, if you ask me, does not party with us all often and keeps himself to himself and thinks he is above us all."

The other laughed quietly.

"Yeah," he replied. "Doesn't seem to party like the rest of us."

I stood there for a moment, pretending to study the rows of bottles behind the bar as though I hadn't heard anything at all.

It wasn't exactly an insult. In truth, it was more an observation than anything else, but it confirmed something I had already begun to sense.

I didn't quite fit the mould of the party brigade of reps.

When I returned to the table, the conversation had moved on, and nobody seemed aware that I had overheard them. And if I'm honest, it didn't bother me as much as it might have done. If anything, it simply reinforced what I was already beginning to understand about myself.

After another half hour or so, the noise of the bar began to feel heavier, the music louder and the conversations less interesting. Eventually I stood up from the table.

"Heading off already?" Alison asked, glancing up from her drink.

I smiled slightly.

"Early start tomorrow," I said.

She raised an eyebrow, clearly aware that this was only partly true.

"Go on then," she said with a small grin. "Don't get lost exploring the island again. If you want company, then I'd be happy to join you, sweetie."

"Well," I replied, "I was thinking of catching a Taxi into Palma for a wander and drink maybe."

She didn't hesitate.

"Give me two minutes," she said, finishing the last of her drink and setting the glass down on the table.

We stepped out of the bar together into the warm night air. The music from inside faded quickly as we walked along the promenade, the sound of the sea gently replacing it.

We jumped into a Taxi, and before long, we were sitting quietly beside each other on the short journey into Palma. Neither of us spoke very much. There was something comfortable in the silence, the sort that doesn't need filling.

When we arrived, the old city felt peaceful in a way that the resort never quite managed. Sure, it had its red light district, if you could call it that, but nothing bad. Narrow streets lay under the soft glow of the lamps, and the distant murmur of conversation drifted out from the occasional late-night café.

Eventually, we wandered down toward the cathedral. La Seu stood silently against the night sky, its vast stone walls illuminated softly from below. Even after seeing it before, the scale of it always made you stop for a moment.

We walked slowly along the nearby waterfront before finding a quiet place to sit overlooking the sea. The harbour lights shimmered across the water, and above us, the sky was clear, scattered with stars.

Alison leaned back slightly, looking upward.

"You know," she said softly, "most people back home would never believe this is our normal life."

I followed her gaze toward the sky.

"It doesn't feel normal," I replied. "It feels like we've somehow slipped into another world."

She smiled at that and rested her head lightly against my shoulder.

For a few minutes, we simply sat there in comfortable silence, listening to the quiet movement of the water and watching the stars above the cathedral towers.

It was a very different moment from the noise and energy of the bars back in Palma Nova. And in that quiet space, I realised something else about the strange life we were living out there on the island.

Sometimes the most memorable parts of it weren't the parties or the stories that everyone else talked about. Sometimes it was simply sitting under a Mediterranean sky with someone who understood the experience as deeply as you did.

And in that moment, with Alison beside me and the warm Mallorcan night stretching quietly around us, I felt very far from the life I had left behind in England.

In truth, I wasn't sure I wanted to go back, but I knew, unbeknownst to Alison, that my stay on this island was not as long as theirs; I would at some point be heading back to head office.

We sat there for quite some time, neither of us feeling any particular need to move or say very much. Occasionally, a car passed quietly along the road behind us, but otherwise the city had settled into that calm rhythm that only seems to arrive late at night.

Eventually, Alison straightened slightly and looked back toward the cathedral, its great stone walls glowing softly under the lights.

"It's funny," she said after a moment. "People think we're just out here having one long party."

I smiled.

"A lot of them are," I replied.

She laughed quietly at that and nudged my arm.

"But not you," she said.

I thought about it for a moment before answering.

"No," I said slowly. "Not really."

The truth was that I was beginning to realise something about myself that perhaps others had already noticed before I had. While many of the other reps were fully embracing the energy of the resort life, the bars, the late nights, the constant social circle, I seemed to be drifting toward something slightly different. What fascinated me about Mallorca wasn't just the holiday scene.

It was the island itself.

The old streets of Palma. The quiet villages hidden in the mountains. The small cafés where locals talked late into the evening, while the tourists had long since gone back to their hotels.

It felt as though the island had layers, and the further you wandered away from the obvious places, the more it slowly revealed them.

Alison seemed to understand that without me needing to explain it fully.

After a while, we began the slow walk back toward the Taxi rank, the streets still quiet and the warm air carrying that soft Mediterranean scent of sea and stone.

As the Taxi carried us back toward Palma Nova, I sat looking out of the window at the dark outline of the coastline passing by.

In later years, I would often look back on that early period of my travel career and realise just how important those small moments had been. At the time, they simply felt like quiet evenings or chance conversations, nothing particularly remarkable.

But slowly, almost without noticing it, the island and the people I met there were beginning to shape something deeper.

They were shaping the person I was becoming.

And although I didn't fully understand it yet, Mallorca was already leaving its mark on my life in ways that would stay with me long after that time had ended.

Chapter Nine

As the weeks passed, life in Mallorca began to settle into a rhythm that, at first, had seemed almost impossible to imagine.

In the early days, everything had felt unfamiliar and slightly uncertain. The pace of the work, the personalities of the guests, and the constant small decisions that had to be made throughout each day. But gradually, the job began to make sense in a way that only experience can. The routines that had once felt overwhelming slowly became second nature, and the island itself began to feel less like a place I was visiting and more like somewhere I truly belonged.

Most mornings started early, long before many of the holidaymakers had even begun to think about breakfast. The air in Palma Nova at that hour was often beautifully still, the sea lying flat and glassy beneath the rising sun. I would walk along the promenade toward whichever unit I was visiting that morning, clipboard in hand, passing the occasional café owner preparing tables for the day ahead or a hotel cleaner hosing down the pavement outside their entrance.

There was something peaceful about those early walks. The resort, which only a few hours earlier had been alive with music and laughter, seemed to pause for a brief moment before the next day began. For a young rep learning the ropes, those quiet moments provided a chance to collect your thoughts before the steady stream of questions and problems inevitably arrived.

Morning surgeries in the hotel receptions quickly became the centrepiece of the day. Guests would drift in with their queries, sometimes small and sometimes rather more complicated. Lost keys, excursion questions, restaurant recommendations, requests for extra towels, and occasionally something more serious that required careful handling. By that stage, I had already learned that half the job of being a rep was simply listening patiently and reassuring people that whatever problem they had encountered could be solved.

Most of the time, it could.

After the morning visits, there were usually excursions to organise or paperwork waiting back at the office. Coaches would arrive along the promenade, engines humming quietly while guests climbed aboard with cameras, sunhats and a sense of anticipation for whatever part of the island they were about to discover that day. Sometimes I travelled with them, guiding the trip and sharing stories about Mallorca. Other times, my role was simply to see them safely on their way before continuing with the endless small tasks that kept the operation running.

Afternoons in the resort had their own distinct character. The sun sat high and strong in the sky, the beaches filled with families, and the cafés buzzing with conversation in half a dozen different languages. For the rep, it was often a strange mixture of activity and waiting. checking arrivals, following up on guest issues, speaking with hotel managers, or simply walking the resort to make sure everything was running smoothly.

By evening, the energy shifted once again.

Holidaymakers returned from the beach sunburnt and content, restaurants filled with laughter and the smell of grilled fish drifting through the streets. This was the time when many reps came into their element, leading welcome meetings, organising events or guiding guests through the nightlife of the resort.

For me, those evenings were often something quieter.

Of course, there were nights spent with the team, sharing drinks and stories after a long day, but more and more I found myself slipping away from the noise and visiting places. Other times it meant simply walking along the coastline, listening to the waves roll gently against the shore while the lights of the resort shimmered across the water.

The island had begun to reveal itself to me slowly, almost as though it rewarded curiosity.

Beyond the busy beaches and lively bars, there was another Mallorca altogether. Small villages tucked into the mountains, quiet stone squares where elderly locals sat watching the world pass by, narrow roads winding through olive groves and almond trees that seemed to stretch endlessly across the hills.

Whenever I could, I ventured a little further.

Sometimes alone, sometimes with Alison or one of the other reps who felt the same quiet fascination with the island beyond the resort strip. Those journeys were rarely planned. A bus ride to somewhere unfamiliar, a wrong turning down a small road, or a café discovered by accident could easily turn into an afternoon of exploration.

The more time I spent there, the more Mallorca began to feel less like a destination and more like a teacher.

The job itself was teaching me responsibility, patience and the ability to remain calm when other people were not. But the island was teaching something else entirely. It was teaching me to slow down, to observe the details of the world around me and to appreciate moments that might otherwise have passed unnoticed.

Looking back now, I realise that this was the period when everything began to fall into place.

The job felt natural.

The island felt familiar.

And the young man who had first arrived in Mallorca with a mixture of excitement and uncertainty was slowly discovering that he was becoming something a little different.

A little more confident.

A little more independent.

And perhaps, without fully realising it at the time, someone who was beginning to understand that the experiences of that summer would stay with him for the rest of his life.

A few weeks into the season, I finally found myself with something that had become increasingly rare.

A full day off.

Days like that were precious for reps. The season moved quickly, and most of our time was taken up with guests, excursions and the constant rhythm of resort life. But every now and then, a free day appeared in the schedule, and on this particular morning, I had already decided how I was going to spend it.

I was going to escape the resort and coastline.

Early that morning I walked down to one of the small car rental offices near the promenade and hired the simplest vehicle they had available. It was nothing glamorous, just a small, slightly tired Fiat that had clearly spent most of its life transporting sunburnt tourists around the island.

But for the day it was freedom.

Within half an hour, I was leaving Palma Nova behind, the busy strip of hotels and bars slowly fading in the rear-view mirror as the road carried me inland.

The transformation was surprisingly quick.

The familiar resort scenery gave way to quieter roads and open countryside. Olive groves stretched across the hillsides, their silvery leaves catching the morning sunlight. Small stone houses appeared occasionally between the fields, many of them looking as though they had stood there for generations.

The further I drove, the more it felt as though I was slowly stepping into another Mallorca altogether.

Tourists rarely ventured far beyond the beaches and the popular excursion routes, yet only a short distance away, the island revealed a completely different personality. Here, life moved at a slower, older pace.

Eventually, the road began to climb. Ahead of me the Serra de Tramuntana mountains rose gradually from the landscape, their rugged slopes stretching along the western edge of the island like a great natural wall protecting the coastline beyond.

The drive itself became an experience.

The road twisted and curved through the mountains, sometimes revealing wide open views across valleys filled with terraces of olive trees, sometimes narrowing into tight bends that forced the small Fiat to slow almost to a crawl.

Every now and then, I would pull the car to the side of the road simply to stand and take in the view.

Below me, the island stretched quietly into the distance, small villages dotted across the hillsides and the faint shimmer of the sea far beyond.

It was a Mallorca that most of the visitors staying in Palma Nova would never see.

Eventually, I found myself driving through one of the small mountain villages that seemed almost untouched by tourism. Narrow streets wound between old stone buildings, their wooden shutters half closed against the warmth of the day. A few elderly locals sat quietly outside a café in the central square, watching the world pass by with the calm patience of people who had lived there their entire lives.

I parked the car and wandered slowly through the village on foot.

There was no rush, no crowds and no souvenir shops trying to attract passing tourists. Instead, there were small bakeries, a local bar where a handful of men stood talking quietly, and the distant sound of church bells echoing gently across the valley.

I eventually found a small café and sat outside with a simple coffee, watching the slow rhythm of village life unfold around me.

It struck me then how different this Mallorca was from the one most visitors believed they knew.

For them the island meant beaches, sangria and lively nights along the resort strip.

But here in the mountains, there was something else entirely.

History.

Tradition.

A way of life that had existed long before the arrival of tour operators and package holidays.

As I sat there in the warm morning sun, listening to the quiet conversations drifting from the nearby tables, I felt a deep sense of gratitude for the strange path that had brought me there.

Working as a rep had brought me to Mallorca, but it was moments like this that made the experience truly meaningful.

Because beyond the work, beyond the guests and the busy life of the resort, there was an island waiting quietly to be discovered.

And on that day, driving alone through the Tramuntana mountains with no particular destination in mind, I felt as though I had been allowed to glimpse the real Mallorca, the one that existed long before the holiday brochures arrived.

It was beautiful.

And in its quiet, understated way, it left a deeper impression on me than any beach or nightclub ever could.

As I sat there with my coffee, watching the quiet life of the village unfold around me, I became aware that someone had taken the table beside mine.

He was an elderly Mallorcan man, perhaps in his seventies or even older. His skin had the deep, weathered look of someone who had spent most of his life under the Mediterranean sun, and his hands rested heavily on the small wooden table as though they carried the memory of many years of work.

He nodded politely in my direction.

"Buenos días," he said.

"Buenos días," I replied, grateful to share some words of Spanish.

For a few moments we both simply sat quietly, drinking our coffee and watching the slow movement of the village square. Eventually he gestured gently toward the car parked nearby.

"You are visiting?" he asked in careful, deliberate Spanish.

"Yes," I said. "I work in Palma Nova."

He smiled at that, the sort of knowing smile that suggested he had seen many young foreigners arrive on the island over the years.

"Tourismo," he said, nodding slowly.

"Yes," I replied.

He looked around the square for a moment, taking in the stone buildings and the quiet rhythm of the morning before speaking again.

"Mallorca is very different there," he said, gesturing vaguely in the direction of the coast.

I understood exactly what he meant.

"Yes," I said. "Very different."

He chuckled softly and lifted his small glass of coffee before taking another sip.

"For us," he said, placing the glass back on the table, "this is Mallorca."

His hand moved slowly around the square, pointing out the church, the café, the narrow streets that disappeared between the old stone houses.

Then he pointed toward the mountains rising behind the village.

"My father worked those terraces," he said quietly. "Olives. Always olives."

I followed his gaze toward the hillsides where rows of ancient olive trees stretched across the slopes.

It was suddenly easy to imagine generations of families living and working in that landscape long before the island had become a holiday destination.

"Many visitors come to Mallorca," he continued after a moment. "But they do not see Mallorca."

The simplicity of the statement struck me.

I nodded slowly.

"I think you are right."

He smiled again, this time with a quiet warmth that seemed to carry a lifetime of experience.

"You see a little," he said.

For a while we sat in comfortable silence again, two strangers sharing the same quiet corner of the village square.

Eventually he stood up slowly, nodded once more, and placed a few coins on the table.

"Disfruta la isla," he said gently.

Enjoy the island.

With that he walked slowly across the square and disappeared into one of the narrow streets between the houses.

I remained there for a few minutes longer, finishing my coffee and reflecting on the simple conversation we had just shared.

It had lasted no more than ten minutes.

Yet somehow it seemed to capture something important about the island and truthfully stayed with me all my life. Mallorca wasn't just the beaches and the holiday resorts that filled the brochures back in Britain.

It was villages like this.

Old men who had spent their lives working the land.

Stone streets that had seen centuries pass quietly by.

And as I eventually stood up, leaving a few coins on the table and making my way back toward the small car waiting by the edge of the square, I realised that the island was slowly revealing itself to me in ways that many visitors never experienced.

Not through excursions or organised tours.

But through small, quiet moments like that one.

Moments that stayed with you long after the journey was over.

The village had returned to its quiet rhythm. The same elderly men still sat outside the café, speaking softly to one another, while somewhere in the distance the church bell sounded the hour. Nothing seemed hurried there, as though time itself moved more gently among those stone streets.

I started the small Fiat and eased it slowly back onto the narrow road that wound its way out of the village and into the mountains once again.

For a while the road continued to climb, twisting steadily through the rocky slopes of the Tramuntana mountain range. Pine trees leaned across the bends, their scent drifting through the open window, while the engine of the little car worked patiently against the incline.

Driving those mountain roads demanded your full attention. The bends appeared suddenly and often sharply, revealing new views at every turn. Sometimes the road clung closely to the hillside, with stone terraces rising above it where olive trees had grown for generations. At other times, the landscape opened wide, offering sweeping views across valleys that seemed to stretch endlessly toward the horizon.

Eventually, the road began its descent.

The mountains slowly loosened their grip on the landscape, the curves of the road softening as it wound its way downward toward the coast.

And then it happened.

At one particular bend, the view suddenly opened completely.

Beyond the last ridge of mountains, the Mediterranean Sea appeared, vast and shimmering beneath the afternoon sun. The water stretched out in a deep, endless blue, meeting the sky somewhere far beyond the horizon.

I instinctively slowed the car and pulled over at the side of the road.

For a moment, I simply sat there, looking out across the view.

It was one of those scenes that seemed almost unreal in its beauty. The rugged mountains behind me, the terraced hillsides falling away toward the coast, and beyond it all the open sea glowing under the warm Mallorcan light.

It struck me then how extraordinary the island truly was.

Only an hour earlier, I had been sitting quietly in a mountain village where life moved slowly, and tradition still shaped everyday existence. Now, just a few bends further down the road, the Mediterranean stretched endlessly before me.

Few places seemed capable of holding such different worlds so closely together.

After a while I started the engine again and continued the descent, the road gradually guiding me back toward the coastline and eventually the familiar resort towns that lined the bay.

But something about that moment stayed with me.

Perhaps it was the conversation with the old Mallorcan man in the café, or perhaps it was simply the quiet beauty of the mountains themselves.

Either way, as the sea slowly grew larger through the windscreen and the road carried me back toward Palma Nova, I felt certain of one thing.

Mallorca had already begun to weave itself quietly into my life. And I suspected that long after this period on the island had passed, a part of me would always belong to that island.

By the time I reached the outskirts of Palma Nova, the familiar signs of resort life had begun to reappear.

The quiet mountain roads had given way to wider streets lined with hotels and apartment blocks, their balconies dotted with brightly coloured towels drying in the afternoon sun. Holidaymakers wandered slowly along the pavements in shorts and sandals, many of them carrying inflatable beach toys or cameras, their skin already beginning to show the first deep glow of a Mediterranean tan.

The air itself seemed different.

Where the mountains had carried the scent of pine trees and warm stone, the resort now hummed with the smells of sunscreen, grilled food from nearby restaurants and the faint salty breeze drifting in from the bay.

I drove slowly along the promenade before returning the small Fiat to the rental office where I had picked it up earlier that morning. The young man behind the counter gave the car a quick glance and nodded his approval before scribbling something on a piece of paper and handing back my deposit.

Just like that, my small escape into the mountains was over.

I stepped back out onto the busy Palma Nova and immediately felt the familiar energy of the resort surrounding me once again.

Music drifted from a nearby bar, the sound of laughter spilling out onto the pavement as groups of holidaymakers gathered around small tables. A few children ran past chasing one another while their parents called after them in that mixture of excitement and mild exhaustion that seemed to define family holidays.

It was the Mallorca that most visitors came to see. And yet, after the quiet villages and mountain roads of the Tramuntana, it somehow felt slightly different to me now.

Not worse.

Just different.

Standing there for a moment, watching the steady flow of holidaymakers moving along the beach, I realised how strange the contrast between those two worlds really was. Only a short drive separated them, yet they seemed to exist in entirely different realities.

In one, the island lived quietly among olive trees and stone houses, its rhythms shaped by generations of tradition.

In the other, it pulsed with the bright energy of tourism, laughter and the carefree optimism of people enjoying their precious weeks in the sun.

And somewhere between those two worlds was where I now found myself.

A young overseas rep learning the job, guiding visitors through the Mallorca they expected to see, while slowly discovering a much deeper island beyond it.

As I walked back toward the hotel that evening, the sun beginning its slow descent toward the horizon, I felt a quiet sense of balance beginning to settle into my life on the island.

The work, the people, the places I was discovering.

All of it was slowly forming the rhythm of a time in Mallorca that I knew, even then, would remain with me for many years to come.

131

Chapter Ten

It was during one of my occasional afternoons wandering through Palma that something completely unexpected caught my eye.

I had been walking slowly along one of the streets near the harbour, enjoying the quiet energy of the city as it moved through the late afternoon towards early evening. The old town carried a very different atmosphere to the resorts. Narrow streets twisted between tall stone buildings, small cafés spilled softly onto the pavements, and the scent of cooking drifted out from open restaurant doors.

Then I saw it.

A small car pulled up near the side of the road, the sort of slightly battered vehicle that looked as though it had seen plenty of miles along Mallorca's winding roads.

What caught my attention immediately, however, was what was strapped to the roof.

Two surfboards.

For a moment I simply stopped and stared, almost unsure that what I was seeing was real.

Surfboards were not something you expected to see very often in Mallorca. The island was famous for its beaches and clear water, but surfing was rarely mentioned in the holiday brochures and as a surfer I really had not seen much sign of waves.

Curiosity quickly took over.

I walked across the street and approached the car just as the two men inside stepped out.

They were clearly locals, both sun-browned and relaxed in the easy way that surfers often are. One of them noticed me looking at the boards and smiled.

"You surf?" he asked in English.

"Yes," I replied immediately. "Back home in England."

That seemed to please them.

Within minutes, we were standing beside the car talking about waves, my boards and the boards on the car and the different surf spots around Europe. Their names were Miguel and Javier, both Mallorcan surfers who spent most of their free time chasing waves around the island.

They laughed when I told them I was working as an overseas rep in Palma Nova.

"You have waves here, too," Miguel said with a grin.

"Not many people know."

They explained that while Mallorca wasn't known internationally as a surfing destination, the island actually received swell from several directions during the spring, autumn and winter months and even occasional summer systems. When the conditions were right, waves could appear along parts of the eastern and northern coastline.

"Maybe one hundred and seventy days a year," Javier said proudly.

I raised an eyebrow at that.

"Really?"

He nodded confidently.

"Sometimes small, sometimes bigger, but always something if you know where to look."

Before long they were telling me about places I had never heard of, Cala Mesquida, Cala Torta, Son Serra and several other beaches scattered along the wild northern coast of the island.

They had spare boards too.

"You call us next time you have a day off," Miguel said, pulling a small piece of paper from his pocket and writing down a telephone number.

"We go find waves."

I folded the paper carefully and placed it in my wallet.

"Deal," I said.

A few weeks later, that opportunity arrived.

I had just finished a busy week when the schedule finally delivered another rare gift.

A full day off.

The first thing I did was find a telephone.

I dialled the number Miguel had given me and waited.

He answered almost immediately.

"You are lucky," he said after I explained who was calling.

"There are waves today."

Less than an hour later, I was standing in the reception area of the Santa Lucia hotel when a dusty white Suzuki jeep pulled up outside.

Three surfboards were already strapped across the back.

Miguel leaned out of the driver's window and waved.

I grabbed my small bag and hurried across the reception.

A couple of the other reps were sitting near the bar and looked up as I passed.

"Where are you off to?" one of them called.

I didn't slow down.

"Surfing," I replied over my shoulder.

Alison appeared in the doorway just in time to see me jump into the jeep.

She laughed and shook her head as Miguel pulled away from the hotel and accelerated down the road. For most of the reps it must have seemed like a completely different side of me.

The quiet rep who often wandered off alone, exploring the island, was suddenly racing away in a jeep with surfboards strapped to the back.

But in truth, this was a side of myself that had always been there. Surfing had been part of my life long before Mallorca entered the picture.

And now, somehow, the island had revealed yet another secret.

The drive north took us through landscapes that felt far removed from the busy resort strip.

Fields stretched across the countryside, small villages appeared between rolling hills, and gradually the road carried us toward the wilder eastern coastline of the island.

Eventually, we reached Cala Mesquida.

The beach opened wide before us, framed by dunes and low hills that seemed untouched by the kind of development found in the resorts. The wind moved softly across the sand and the sea beyond rolled in long, steady lines.

Waves.

Not enormous ones, but clean, playful waves breaking gently across the bay.

Miguel grinned as we stepped out of the jeep.

"You see?" he said.

"Mallorca has surf."

We waxed the boards and walked down toward the water.

Standing there with the Mediterranean stretching out before me, board under my arm and the warm island sun on my back, I felt the same quiet excitement that every surfer recognises.

The promise of a wave.

And as we paddled out together beyond the breaking surf, I realised that Mallorca had once again revealed something unexpected.

Another hidden side of the island.

One that very few visitors ever discover.

I sat for a while in the lineup, gently bobbing in the water with only a handful of other surfers scattered across the bay. One of the first things you learn when surfing somewhere unfamiliar is to respect the locals, so I simply nodded to the others and waited my turn. A few sets rolled through, and I let them take the first waves, watching quietly as they paddled, stood and rode toward the beach.

Like an expensive cork, I floated there rising and falling with the movement of the sea, waiting patiently.

Then it came.

A clean set rolled toward us, slightly more on my side of the lineup. I turned the Malibu board toward the beach and began paddling with a few strong strokes. Almost immediately I felt the board lift beneath me as the wave picked me up and pushed me forward.

In one smooth motion I jumped to my feet.

I was surfing in Mallorca.

For a moment it felt almost surreal. The warm Mediterranean water, the sun shining across the bay and the small but perfectly shaped wave carrying me toward the shore. I dropped slightly into a crouch and rode along the face of the wave, gliding across the water in that effortless way that surfers always dream about. For a few seconds I felt exactly like one of those pelicans you see skimming across the waves along the Californian coastline.

Then the wave began to fade near the beach, and I kicked out into the water.

What a ride.

As I paddled back out toward the lineup I realised, I had a huge grin across my face.

Miguel was sitting on his board further out and raised his arm in the air with a broad smile of his own. I suspect he was simply happy to have another surfer out there sharing the waves with him.

And that was the start of a four-hour surfing session.

The waves were not large, but they were clean, playful and consistent enough to keep us in the water for most of the afternoon. Wave after wave rolled through the bay while the small group of surfers took turns enjoying the ride.

Eventually, exhausted but completely satisfied, we paddled back toward the beach.

It was only when I stepped onto the sand that I realised something rather important.

In my excitement to get into the water I had completely forgotten about one small but essential detail.

Sun cream.

Without any doubt I was burning and burning badly. My shoulders felt raw, my nose was beginning to sting fiercely, and I could already feel the unmistakable heat of a serious sunburn building across my skin.

Miguel took one look at me and shook his head.

"You English," he laughed.

Then he walked over to a nearby cactus plant growing beside the dunes. Pulling a large knife from the jeep, he carefully cut off one of the thick green paddles and sliced it open.

Inside was a cool, clear gel.

He brought the pieces back and began placing the cactus flesh gently across my shoulders and nose.

The relief was immediate.

The cool gel soothed the burning skin and for a few minutes I simply stood there on the beach covered in pieces of cactus while Miguel and Javier laughed at my obvious mistake.

It was, as I was about to learn, a very practical island remedy.

Still, I knew I was in trouble.

By the time we began the drive back across the island I could feel the first signs of sunstroke creeping in. My skin throbbed under the heat of the burn and my head felt slightly heavy from the long hours under the Mediterranean sun.

Yet despite that, I couldn't stop smiling.

The day had been incredible.

Surfing in Mallorca had been something I had never expected, and even now, many years later, the memory of that first wave still feels a little magical.

By the time we reached the Santa Lucia hotel the sun was beginning to lower across the bay.

As I stepped out of the jeep, still with pieces of cactus resting across my shoulders, Alison happened to be walking through the reception area.

She stopped instantly when she saw me.

"Damn, Wesley," she said, looking me up and down with clear concern. "You are in trouble."

I laughed weakly.

"Yes," I admitted. "It's bad."

She shook her head, examining my shoulders and nose.

"That cactus might be helping," she said, "but we need to get you to the clinic immediately."

Within minutes Alison had guided me out of the hotel and into a taxi bound for the local clinic. By this stage the adrenaline from the day was beginning to wear off and the reality of what I had done to myself was becoming painfully obvious.

The doctor didn't take long to make his diagnosis.

Severe sunburn, combined with the early signs of sunstroke.

He examined my shoulders and nose carefully before shaking his head in that slow, slightly disapproving way that doctors sometimes do when they know exactly what has caused the problem.

"No sol," he said firmly, raising a finger for emphasis.

For several days.

That instruction alone was enough to make me wince almost as much as the burn itself. For a young overseas rep working in the middle of a Mallorcan summer, avoiding the sun was easier said than done.

Still, the orders were clear.

Cool showers, soothing creams, and, most importantly, staying out of the sun while my skin recovered.

The next few days were not my finest professional moment.

While the other reps carried on with their normal duties, excursions and welcome meetings, I spent most of my time moving slowly between the shade of my room and brief appearances at the hotel reception, trying to avoid the sun like a vampire hiding from daylight.

The burn across my shoulders gradually turned from angry red to something slightly more manageable, though not without peeling in a way that made me look rather less like a confident young man and more like someone who had lost a fight with the Mediterranean sun.

My colleagues, of course, found the whole situation highly amusing.

Stories of my surfing adventure quickly travelled through the small network of reps working across the resorts. A few of them congratulated me on finding waves in Mallorca at all, something many had never even considered possible. Others simply laughed at the fact that I had managed to incapacitate myself for several days by forgetting the most basic rule of spending time under the Mediterranean sun.

Alison, meanwhile, took a slightly more sympathetic approach.

Although she did not miss the opportunity to tease me about my foolishness, she also made sure I was properly looked after while I recovered. More than once, she appeared with cold drinks or a fresh layer of soothing cream for my shoulders, shaking her head in quiet disbelief at the whole episode.

"You travelled all the way to Mallorca to burn yourself to a crisp," she said one evening with a grin.

"Surfing," I corrected gently.

"Surfing," she repeated, laughing.

Looking back now, the whole incident feels almost inevitable.

I had discovered waves on an island that most people never associated with surfing, spent hours in the water enjoying the simple joy of riding those unexpected Mediterranean swells, and paid the price for my enthusiasm by forgetting the most basic protection against the sun.

But despite the discomfort and the few days of embarrassment that followed, I never once regretted that day.

Because in those few hours out in the water, I had discovered something else about Mallorca.

The island still had secrets.

Hidden waves along its wild coastlines, quiet mountain villages untouched by tourism, and small moments of connection with people and places that most visitors would never experience.

And if the price of discovering that side of the island was a badly sunburnt pair of shoulders and a few days away from the sun, then it was a lesson I was more than willing to accept.

It was, without doubt, my first real lesson about surfing in warm climates.

And certainly not my last.

Chapter Eleven

I waited along the promenade for the coach that would take me to Palma Airport for the afternoon transfers. The day was warm and pleasant, around twenty-seven degrees, and there was that subtle feeling in the air that summer was not far away. Mallorca was beginning to shift into a different gear. The island seemed to sense the coming season long before the official holiday timetables declared it.

I had already completed a number of airport transfers during my time as a rep, but normally, there were dedicated transfer reps who handled most of that side of the operation. It was demanding work, requiring patience, organisation and a certain tolerance for chaos, especially when flights arrived close together.

However, one of the transfer reps had recently left and returned home, which meant the rest of us were stepping in to cover the duties until a replacement arrived. Alison had mentioned earlier that Stephanie would also be working at the airport that afternoon, as the schedule was particularly busy.

It was one of those strange transitional periods in the season when the final low and mid-season flights were still operating while the early summer schedules were beginning to ramp up. For Mallorca, that meant a noticeable increase in arrivals from across the United Kingdom. More airports, more flights and, inevitably, more guests arriving within short periods of time.

The coach soon appeared along the road and pulled in beside the pavement. I climbed aboard and greeted the driver before taking a seat near the front as we made our way toward Palma.

From the window I watched the coastline slip by, the familiar stretch of hotels, cafés and small beach bars slowly giving way to the wider roads that carried traffic toward the capital and the airport beyond.

Alison had already briefed me on the plan for the afternoon that the office had advised.

Stephanie would be looking after the arrivals coming in from London Gatwick, which were always among the busiest flights. My responsibility would begin once I had dropped off the departing passengers. After that I would remain at the airport to handle the arrivals coming in from East Midlands.

Truth be told, I was rather looking forward to it.

Airport duty was never dull. You met people arriving for the start of their holidays, full of excitement and anticipation, and at the same time you dealt with guests heading home, often tired, sunburnt and reluctant to leave the island behind.

Somewhere between those two groups stood the overseas reps, quietly making sure everything ran as smoothly as possible.

At least, that was the plan.

What none of us realised at that moment was that Palma Airport was about to deliver one of those long, exhausting days that every overseas rep eventually experiences.

Hotel collections can sometimes pass by without incident, but on other occasions they can prove surprisingly testing. One of the things you quickly learn as an overseas rep is that many guests believe their situation is somehow more important than everyone else's.

There will always be the late ones.

The guests who stroll down to the coach at a snail's pace while everyone else waits patiently on board. Others suddenly remember they may have left something in their room just as the luggage has been loaded. Occasionally someone will even panic about a missing passport, only for it to be discovered moments later sitting quietly inside the very bag they are holding.

The small delays are endless.

After a while, however, you learn to take it all in your stride. Patience becomes part of the job.

This particular day was no different, though it did feel as though we had encountered more "go slow" passengers than usual. It wasn't really an age thing either. Sometimes a group simply seems to move at half the speed of normal life.

That morning, I felt as though I was operating at full speed while everyone else appeared to be moving through treacle.

By the time we reached the final accommodation unit for collection, the driver glanced across at me and raised his eyebrows with a knowing expression.

We had somehow managed to bleed twenty-five minutes in delays.

That meant we were now running behind schedule, and the gentle pace of the collections suddenly gave way to a much more focused drive toward the airport.

Fortunately, Palma Airport is relatively close to the resorts of Palma Nova and Magaluf, so even with the lost time we still had a good chance of arriving before things became critical, as long as no delays in Palma city itself we would be fine.

Still, as the coach accelerated along the road toward Palma, it was clear that the afternoon was already beginning to develop a slightly more hurried tone than we had planned.

And we had not even reached the airport yet.

I remember there was a rather annoying young boy sitting behind me on the coach that day.

His parents seemed perfectly content to let him entertain himself however he wished, which unfortunately meant he had discovered that poking a plastic pirate sword through the gap in the seats was a particularly amusing activity. Every few moments, the tip of the sword would appear somewhere near the side of my head before quickly disappearing again.

At first, I smiled politely, turning slightly to acknowledge him in the hope that the novelty might wear off.

It didn't.

After ten minutes of this unexpected fencing lesson, the situation was becoming increasingly irritating. The boy seemed to find the whole thing endlessly entertaining, while his parents remained blissfully unaware of the small battle taking place just inches behind my seat.

Still, part of the job was learning to remain calm in situations that might otherwise test your patience. So, I continued to smile, though admittedly not quite as enthusiastically as before.

Eventually, the coach rolled into the airport coach bays at Palma, and the small sword attacks finally came to an end.

I stepped off the coach and began organising the offload of passengers and luggage, helping guests gather their belongings and directing them toward the terminal entrance. Once everyone was safely inside I confirmed the next arrangements with the driver before turning my attention toward the check-in desks.

It was then that the senior airport rep approached me.

He greeted me warmly but almost immediately pulled me slightly to one side, lowering his voice as he spoke.

"We've got problems," he said quietly.

He explained that delays had already begun to build across the airport and that the situation was likely to become much worse as the afternoon progressed.

Spanish air traffic controllers had apparently begun industrial action earlier that morning without much warning. On top of that, severe weather was moving across France and parts of the United Kingdom, which meant aircraft movements throughout Western Europe were already backing up.

Flights were beginning to stack, departures were slowing down, and arrival times were slipping further behind schedule by the hour.

"We'll check the guests in as normal," he said, "but it's looking like four to six hour delays at least."

He paused for a moment before adding the part that would make the day considerably more complicated.

"There's a strong chance we'll have to take them airside to wait, have you got your passport with you?" I had been told to bring my passport by Alison before I left, just in case, but I had not really questioned it. "Yes, Alison told me to bring it." He smiled, happy with that.

In those days, the situation was even more challenging because information travelled slowly. There was no internet, no instant updates appearing on mobile phones or airport apps. News was moved by word of mouth, telephone calls and the occasional announcement over the airport loudspeakers.

Which meant that, for the moment at least, the only people who really understood how difficult the afternoon was about to become were the airport staff… and the overseas reps trying to hold everything together.

And the guests, of course, had absolutely no idea what was coming.

Once the passengers had all passed through check-in and were safely inside the departure area, I made my way over to the airport office desk to see what the latest news was.

What I found there was slightly unexpected.

Several of the other reps were gathered around the desk, leaning casually against the counter, cups of tea and coffee in their hands, laughing and chatting as though nothing particularly dramatic was happening at all.

It was one of those strange scenes you sometimes find in the travel industry, where a potentially serious situation is unfolding but the people dealing with it have already accepted that there is very little, they can do except manage it calmly.

"So, what's the situation?" I asked as I joined them.

John, a rep who worked in another part of Mallorca, looked up and smiled.

"Looks like we've got some serious delays," he said matter-of-factly.

He took another sip of his coffee before continuing.

"We'll probably be heading airside within the next hour. Food and drink vouchers are being organised for the passengers."

I raised an eyebrow.

"Oh damn," I said. "That sounds serious."

John nodded.

"It is."

He explained that the situation was already worse than most passengers realised.

Apparently, none of the aircraft scheduled to arrive from the UK had even left yet.

Not one of them.

The combination of Spanish air traffic control industrial action and severe weather moving across France and the UK had effectively jammed the entire system. Aircraft were waiting on the ground, flight plans were being delayed, and departures were stacking up across several airports.

Which meant that, somewhere in Britain, dozens of aircraft were sitting on runways waiting for permission to depart.

"The airlines' operations team must be having a fun afternoon," John added with a grin.

"And head office too, I imagine."

I nodded slowly as the reality of the situation began to settle in.

If the aircraft hadn't even left the UK yet, then the passengers already sitting in Palma Airport had a very long wait ahead of them.

And for the overseas reps, that meant the afternoon was about to become considerably more complicated.

As I stood there listening to the growing discussion about delays and vouchers, I suddenly noticed someone walking past in a Dan Air uniform.

For a moment, I wasn't quite sure if my eyes were playing tricks on me.

Then I recognised her. An old school friend!

"Hey!" I shouted across the terminal.

She turned immediately, and the moment she realised who it was, her face broke into a huge grin. Without hesitation, she hurried over and threw her arms around me, greeting me with a warm hug and a quick kiss on the cheek.

"Wesley! Oh, my goodness!"

We both laughed.

"So lovely to see you," she said. "And wow… look at us two here in Palma!"

I shook my head slightly, still surprised by the chance encounter.

"Are you a stewardess now?" I asked.

"Yes!" she replied proudly. "Started a few months ago. It's awesome."

She explained that she had flown into Mallorca the night before and had overnighted on the island with the crew.

"So, you're not affected by all these delays then?" I asked.

She smiled.

"Oh, we are," she said. "Nobody's going anywhere just yet."

Apparently, the crew had been asked to return to the aircraft and prepare it just in case they received clearance to depart at short notice.

"I hope you're well," she said quickly, glancing back toward the terminal where several other crew members were gathering near passport control.

"I must dash, Wesley. But hopefully we'll meet again someday… somewhere at another airport!"

And just like that, she hurried off to join her colleagues, disappearing into the busy flow of passengers and airport staff.

I stood there for a moment watching her go, smiling at the strange way life sometimes reconnects people in the most unexpected places.

The sad truth, however, is that I never saw her again.

Not once.

The last I ever heard was that she left Dan Air in the early 1990s and moved to Europe, where she continued working in aviation, stationed in an airport on the continent.

Strange how paths cross like that in life.

For a brief moment, two people who once knew each other find themselves standing together in an airport on a Mediterranean island… and then the world carries them off in completely different directions again.

Airports, I was beginning to realise, were full of moments like that.

Before long, the senior rep returned and began handing out sheets of paper to each of us. One by one, we took them and clipped them onto our boards. Each sheet contained a list of passenger names along with their flight numbers and hotel details.

It was our working manifest for the evening.

The plan was now clear.

We were going airside.

Airport security had agreed to issue temporary passes so that the reps could move through passport control and into the departure area, where thousands of passengers were already waiting. Our job would be to locate our guests, organise them as best we could and begin distributing food and drink vouchers in the restaurant areas while they waited for news of their delayed flights.

By that point, the delays were already running at three hours.

The latest information suggested that many of the aircraft had still not even left the UK, meaning that arrivals could easily be six hours away. The reality was beginning to sink in.

We were in for a very long night.

It was already seven o'clock in the evening and the situation was becoming increasingly muddled as more information filtered through the airport operations teams. Flights were stacking up across Europe, passengers were gathering in large numbers inside the departure lounges, and the small army of overseas reps was preparing to step into the middle of it all.

Of course, as with any situation involving a large group of reps, there were a few complications.

Several of them had arrived at the airport without their passports.

Even in those days, you could not simply walk airside without proper identification, which meant they were now standing outside the terminal waiting while other resort reps raced across the island in taxis or coaches trying to deliver the missing documents.

A few reps were quietly removed from the airside duty altogether, and replacements were arranged instead.

And sure enough, a short time later, the doors to the terminal opened, and Alison walked in, clearly having just arrived from one of the resorts to take over from another rep who could not stay.

She spotted us almost immediately and waved as she made her way across the hall.

"Well," she said with a small smile as she joined us, "looks like we're in for some fun."

Stephanie laughed.

"That's one way of putting it."

With our clipboards ready and the temporary passes being issued, the three of us began walking together toward passport control.

Beyond those doors waited several thousand delayed passengers. And a very long evening of explaining, organising and calming nerves was about to begin.

It's important to understand that it wasn't just British passengers affected by the delays that evening.

Across the departure lounge, there were travellers from all over Europe. French, German, Scandinavian and Dutch holidaymakers were all caught in the same situation, their flights delayed by the same chain of events stretching across the continent.

The result was a departure area that was becoming increasingly crowded by the minute.

Even at the best of times, Palma Airport struggled slightly with seating in the main waiting areas, but now thousands of delayed passengers had flooded into the departure lounges all at once. Families sat on the floor, couples leaned against walls, and groups gathered around the limited restaurant tables, hoping to secure somewhere comfortable to wait.

The atmosphere was not yet tense, but it was certainly restless.

People had begun to realise that something was wrong.

Palma Airport at that time was not particularly large by modern standards. It certainly had shops and restaurants, but nothing like the scale of the major international airports many travellers are familiar with today. The facilities simply were not designed to accommodate thousands of delayed passengers all at once.

A few cafés and small restaurants did their best to cope with the sudden surge of customers, but queues were already forming, and tables were filling quickly.

It was becoming clear that the airport was not really geared up for the kind of large-scale disruption we were now facing.

And somewhere among those thousands of passengers were our guests.

Our job, as overseas reps, was to find them, organise them as best we could and try to keep everyone calm while the long evening slowly unfolded.

The evening seemed to stretch endlessly.

For hours, the departure lounges had been filled with tired passengers clutching vouchers, queues forming at cafés and restaurants while the reps moved constantly between groups of guests trying to keep everyone informed and calm.

Eventually, however, the long wait began to move toward its next stage.

Shortly after eleven o'clock that night, the first aircraft from the United Kingdom finally began to arrive.

Word spread quickly across the airport operations desks and through the small army of overseas reps who had been working the terminals all evening. The London flight was the first to touch down, and fortunately for me, the East Midlands aircraft was scheduled to land only ten minutes later.

It was a small piece of luck in what had otherwise been a very long day.

The Glasgow and Manchester flights, however, were still several hours behind schedule and were not expected to arrive for at least another two hours.

For the reps responsible for those passengers, the night was far from over.

Fortunately for Alison, Stephanie and me, our flights were among the first wave, finally making their way into Palma. That meant we could now return to the normal arrivals side of the airport and begin preparing for the next stage of the operation.

After several hours of managing delays and frustrated departure passengers, we now had to switch our attention to welcoming a new group of holidaymakers stepping off aircraft that had spent much of the evening stuck on the ground somewhere in the United Kingdom.

By that point, we knew exactly what to expect.

Passengers arriving after such long delays were rarely in the best of moods. Many would be tired, hungry and slightly irritated after spending hours waiting to depart.

Still, there was always one small advantage waiting for them.

The moment they stepped out of the aircraft and into the warm Mallorcan night air, most people remembered very quickly why they had travelled there in the first place.

And with a bit of luck, the promise of Spanish sunshine waiting for them the next morning would soften the memory of a long and frustrating journey.

By the time the passengers finally began to emerge through the arrivals doors, it was close to midnight.

They looked tired, as you might expect after such a long and frustrating journey, many of them dragging their suitcases behind them with that slightly weary expression travellers often wear after hours spent in airports and aircraft cabins.

Still, one by one, they began to gather around as I called out the hotel names and organised the transfer groups.

Soon enough, we were loading the luggage into the coach and guiding the guests into their seats.

As the coach pulled away from Palma Airport and began the short drive toward the resorts along the coastline, I decided to play some gentle music through the coach system. The soft sounds of the Gipsy Kings drifted quietly through the cabin as the road curved along the bay, the warm Mediterranean night air visible through the windows.

After the long delays and confusion at the airport, the atmosphere on board the coach began to relax surprisingly quickly.

There were ten hotel drop-offs on my route that evening, but to my surprise, the passengers were in remarkably good spirits. Perhaps the worst of the journey was now behind them, or perhaps simply arriving on the island at last had lifted everyone's mood.

Several couples chatted happily about the days ahead, a few families laughed quietly among themselves, and more than once someone leaned forward to ask about the weather forecast for the week.

It turned out to be one of the most pleasant transfers I had ever worked.

Strangely enough, that was not the experience Alison and Stephanie had that night.

When we compared notes the following day, they both complained that their passengers had spent most of the journey moaning about the delays, the long flight and the confusion at the airport.

I could only shrug.

For some reason, my group had arrived in Mallorca full of smiles. Even after the longest of journeys.

Chapter Twelve

By the time the season had settled into its familiar rhythm, I had begun to realise that Mallorca had been teaching me far more than simply how to do the job of an overseas representative.

When I first arrived on the island, everything had felt uncertain. The responsibilities of the role, the expectations of the guests and the constant pace of resort life had seemed overwhelming at times. There had been moments when I wondered whether I truly belonged there at all. Yet slowly, almost without noticing it happening, the island and the people I met there had begun to shape something deeper within me.

Mallorca had quietly become a teacher.

Not in the way a classroom teaches you facts or instructions, but in the much subtler way that life sometimes teaches through experience. Each day presented a different situation, a different challenge, or a different person whose story briefly crossed your own. Some moments were humorous, others were stressful, and a few carried a quiet significance that only became clear much later.

One of the first lessons the island taught me was about people.

Working as a rep meant meeting hundreds of travellers over the course of a season. They arrived with excitement, anticipation and sometimes a little nervousness about being in a foreign country. Many had saved for months, sometimes years, to enjoy a week in the Mediterranean sun. For them the holiday represented something precious, a rare break from work, routine and responsibility.

And when you begin to see things through that perspective, you understand something important about the job.

You are not simply organising transfers or selling excursions.

You are helping to protect someone's special moment.

Of course, not every guest made that easy. There were the impatient ones, the overly demanding ones and the occasional travellers who seemed to believe the world should revolve entirely around their personal holiday plans. Yet even those encounters taught valuable lessons in patience and understanding.

Because beneath the occasional complaints or frustrations, most people simply wanted reassurance that someone was there to help them enjoy their time away.

Another lesson came through responsibility.

Being a rep might appear glamorous from the outside. The sunshine, the beaches and the lively evenings along the resort strip could easily create that impression. But behind that image lay a role that required calm thinking, quick decisions and a steady head when things went wrong.

Lost passports, stolen bags, illness, missed flights, delayed aircraft and anxious guests were all part of the reality of the job. There were moments when situations unfolded quickly and you had to step forward and deal with them without hesitation.

At first those responsibilities felt daunting.

But gradually something changed.

The more situations you handled, the more confidence quietly grew in the background. Problems that once seemed intimidating slowly became manageable. You learned to listen more carefully, to remain calm when others were not, and to find solutions even when the path forward was not immediately clear.

Resilience was another lesson Mallorca offered.

Life as a rep could be exhausting. Long days often stretched into late nights, especially during busy periods when arrivals and departures seemed to blend endlessly into one another. Some days began early with hotel visits and ended long after midnight following airport duties.

Yet strangely, there was a certain energy to it all.

You were young, living abroad, surrounded by new people and experiences that few of your friends back home were likely to encounter. Even the difficult days carried a sense of adventure, because each challenge seemed to add another layer to the experience.

And perhaps the most important lesson Mallorca gave me was something far more personal.

It taught me about myself.

When I first stepped onto the island, I was still discovering who I was becoming as a young man. The world beyond home felt vast and full of possibility, but also slightly intimidating. Living and working abroad forced me to grow in ways that comfort and familiarity never could.

The job demanded independence.

It required confidence.

And sometimes it simply required trusting yourself to handle whatever situation the day happened to present.

Slowly, those qualities began to develop.

Not dramatically, but quietly.

Through hundreds of small moments.

Helping a worried guest find their lost passport. Guiding travellers through the narrow streets of Palma. Sitting in a mountain café listening to an elderly Mallorcan describe the island he had known all his life. Catching an unexpected wave on a hidden beach and feeling the simple joy of riding across the Mediterranean water.

Each of those moments left its mark.

Looking back now, I realise that Mallorca was far more than simply a place where I worked for a season.

It was a place where I learned how to stand on my own two feet.

A place where curiosity and adventure replaced hesitation.

And perhaps most importantly, a place that quietly showed me that the world was far larger, richer and more interesting than I had ever previously imagined.

By the time that season was drawing to its close, I understood something that had not been clear when I first arrived.

Mallorca had not only given me experiences.

It had given me perspective.

And that perspective would stay with me long after the island itself had disappeared from the horizon.

Mallorca also offered something else that I had not fully expected.

It opened a window into a culture and way of life that was very different from the one I had grown up with. Before arriving on the island, my understanding of Spain had been fairly simple, shaped mostly by holiday brochures, travel stories and the occasional glimpse of Mediterranean life through the eyes of tourists on the mainland.

But living there, even for a season, revealed a much deeper picture.

Through the course of the months, I began to learn about the rhythm of Spanish life, the traditions that shaped everyday routines, and the quiet pride that many of the local people carried for their island and its history. Conversations in cafés, chance meetings with locals, and even the occasional visit to the police station while helping guests resolve problems gradually exposed me to a society that operated with its own customs and character.

It was all new to me.

In England, life had always followed a familiar pattern. Here in Mallorca, I was suddenly encountering different languages, different attitudes and different ways of solving problems. Even small things, the pace of daily life, the importance of family gatherings, or the relaxed way many locals approached time itself, offered gentle reminders that the world was far broader than the one I had previously known.

The island also gave me the opportunity to rediscover something that had always been important to me.

The sea.

Finding those hidden surf spots along Mallorca's coastline had been one of the most unexpected gifts of the season. Many

People would never associate the Mediterranean with surfing, yet those quiet beaches where the waves rolled in from distant weather systems provided moments of pure freedom.

Standing on a board in warm water beneath the Mallorcan sun was a feeling that never lost its magic.

It was during those days that I met surfers from the island itself, people who knew the coastline in ways that no guidebook could ever describe. They spoke about hidden coves, changing winds and the small windows of opportunity when the waves arrived. Through them, I discovered yet another layer of Mallorca that most visitors never experience.

But perhaps the most valuable part of that season was simply the people I met along the way.

Guests arriving from across Britain with their own stories and expectations. Fellow reps who became friends through shared experiences, long days and late evenings. Local residents whose lives had been shaped by the island long before tourism arrived.

Each person added something to the experience.

Each conversation, whether brief or meaningful, helped expand my understanding of the world beyond the place I had started from.

Looking back now, I realise how fortunate I was to experience all of this at such an important stage of my life. Many people spend years before discovering the wider world beyond their own surroundings. Mallorca had given me that opportunity early.

And once that door had opened, it was impossible to close again. The island had not simply shown me new places. It had shown me new possibilities.

Perhaps that is the true beauty of travel.

When you first set out for an unfamiliar place, you imagine you are simply visiting somewhere new. You expect to see different landscapes, taste unfamiliar food and hear languages that sound foreign to your ears. Yet somewhere along the way, often without realising it at the time, the journey begins to reveal something much deeper.

Travel has a quiet way of changing you.

It removes the comfort of the familiar and replaces it with curiosity. It introduces you to people whose lives and experiences are completely different from your own, and through those encounters, you slowly begin to see the world with a wider perspective. The boundaries of what once felt normal begin to expand, and the idea of what is possible in life grows with it.

Mallorca had been one of those places.

What began as a season working abroad had become something far more meaningful. The island had offered moments of adventure, moments of responsibility, and moments of simple beauty that seemed almost impossible to forget. From quiet mountain villages and hidden surf beaches to the busy rhythm of resort life and the friendships formed along the way, each experience had added another small piece to the story.

Looking back now, I realise that those months in Mallorca were never really just about a job.

They were about discovery.

Discovery of new places, new cultures, and new people whose paths briefly crossed my own. But perhaps most importantly, they were about discovering a little more about myself and the direction my life might take.

Because once you experience the thrill of stepping into the unknown, of arriving somewhere unfamiliar and slowly uncovering its secrets, something changes within you.

The world begins to feel larger.

And the desire to keep exploring it becomes impossible to ignore.

Another part of the experience that shaped those months was something I had barely thought about at first.

Living in a hotel.

For many guests, a hotel is simply a place you stay for a week or two while on holiday. You check in, unpack your suitcase, enjoy the facilities and eventually return home. But when you live there for an entire season, something quite different begins to happen.

The hotel slowly becomes part of your everyday life.

At the beginning, I was simply another staff member passing through the reception area or the restaurant, someone the guests recognised as the rep responsible for their stay. Yet over time, the rhythm of the hotel itself began to feel familiar. The receptionists would greet you each morning with a nod or a quiet "buenos días." The restaurant staff began to recognise your habits, often placing a coffee or a glass of water on the table before you even asked.

Gradually, you stopped feeling like a visitor.

Instead, you became part of the small community that kept the hotel running each day.

The kitchen staff, the waiters, the cleaners, the night porter who always seemed to know exactly who was coming and going at the oddest hours, they all played their part in the quiet machinery of hotel life. Many of them worked long hours throughout the season, often behind the scenes where guests rarely noticed their efforts.

Yet living among them gave me a new appreciation for how much work went into creating the effortless atmosphere that holidaymakers enjoyed.

It also brought unexpected friendships.

Language barriers existed at times, of course, but those barriers were often overcome with gestures, smiles and the occasional mixture of Spanish and English that somehow managed to communicate enough to keep conversations flowing.

Meals shared late in the evening, quick chats between duties and the occasional drink at the end of a long day all helped create a feeling that the hotel was more than simply a place where people slept.

It had become a kind of temporary family.

And like any family, it had its personalities.

There were those who worked quietly and efficiently behind the scenes, others who seemed to bring humour to even the busiest of days, and a few who had clearly seen many seasons of tourism come and go. From them, you could occasionally hear stories about how Mallorca had changed over the years as more visitors discovered the island.

Listening to those stories made me realise something else.

Although I had arrived thinking of Mallorca as simply a destination for holidaymakers, for the people who lived and worked there, the island was something much deeper. It was home. It was where their families lived, where their traditions continued and where their lives unfolded far beyond the short summer seasons of tourism.

Being welcomed into that environment, even temporarily, was something I came to value deeply.

Because it allowed me to see Mallorca not just through the eyes of a visitor or a tour representative, but through the small daily interactions that revealed the island's true character.

And it was through those quiet connections, often formed in the ordinary moments between duties, that the island began to feel less like somewhere I was working and more like somewhere I belonged, if only for a little while.

Chapter Thirteen

Life as an overseas representative has a curious way of moving forward at its own pace. Days blend into weeks, and weeks slowly shape themselves into a season that begins to feel familiar and almost permanent. Just when that rhythm settles into something comfortable, something unexpected often appears to change the direction of the journey.

For me, that moment arrived quite suddenly.

I had been working through the usual routine of the resort when I was informed that I would be leaving Mallorca sooner than I had anticipated. The company had another role waiting for me back in the United Kingdom, one that required my return within the next few weeks.

The news arrived without much warning.

At first, it felt strange to hear it spoken aloud. Only a short time earlier, I had been settling comfortably into the life I had built on the island. The hotels, the streets of Palma Nova, the familiar faces of the staff and the daily rhythm of the work had all begun to feel normal. Mallorca had quietly become part of my everyday life.

And now, just as suddenly as I had arrived, it seemed the next chapter was calling.

There was no sense of disappointment in the decision itself. Opportunities in the travel industry often appeared unexpectedly, and learning to adapt to them was part of the profession. Yet hearing that I would soon be leaving the island stirred a quiet awareness that the time I had spent there had passed far more quickly than I realised.

The thought of departure had not yet fully settled in my mind.

For the moment, there were still guests to look after, transfers to organise and the familiar routines of resort life to continue. But somewhere in the background, a new awareness had begun to form.

My time in Mallorca was entering its final weeks.

With that knowledge came a subtle shift in the way I looked at the island around me. Places that had become part of my daily routine now carried a slightly different meaning. The walk along the promenade in the evening, the cafés where I often stopped for a quiet coffee, and the hotel reception that had become a second home during the season.

Suddenly, these small moments felt more important.

They were no longer simply part of the routine.

They were becoming memories.

And as the days moved quietly forward, I began to realise that leaving Mallorca would not simply be about finishing a job. It would mean saying goodbye to a place that had quietly changed me in ways I was only just beginning to understand.

I decided that the first people I wanted to tell were Alison and Stephanie.

Over the course of the season, we had become good friends. One of those friendships had grown particularly close, but both of them had shared many of the same experiences that had shaped my time on the island. It felt only right that they should hear the news from me directly.

I arranged to meet them both for dinner in the hotel restaurant that evening.

At the same time, I asked the office to keep the news quiet for the moment. I wanted the chance to speak with the people closest to me before the information began circulating more widely around the resort.

It was a strange mixture of emotions.

Part of me felt genuinely excited about what was ahead. I knew that leaving Mallorca did not mean the end of my career as a rep. In fact, quite the opposite. This was really just the beginning. I had already been told that I would be stepping into another role within the company, covering maternity leave for a few months in the United Kingdom.

It was an opportunity that would broaden my experience and allow me to learn more about the wider workings of the business.

And that knowledge brought a quiet sense of confidence.

Somewhere along the way it had become clear that I was now following a very specific career path within the travel industry. The experiences in Mallorca had not simply been a one-off adventure abroad; they were part of a much larger journey that was only just beginning.

Still, alongside that excitement there was an unmistakable hint of sadness.

Mallorca had become more than simply a workplace during those months. The island had been a classroom, an adventure and a place where friendships had formed in ways that only shared experiences abroad can create.

And of course, there was another small reality waiting for me back in Britain.

The thought of commuting once again through grey skies and unpredictable weather was not quite as appealing as the warm Mediterranean evenings I had grown used to.

But that, I reminded myself with a smile, was all part of the journey.

That evening the hotel restaurant carried the familiar warmth that had become part of daily life during my time on the island. The soft murmur of conversation drifted across the room while the waiters moved between tables with the easy rhythm that comes from long experience. Outside, the last light of the day still lingered across the sea, casting a warm glow through the windows.

Alison arrived first.

She spotted me across the room and walked over with a smile, greeting me with the easy familiarity that had grown between us during the season.

"You sounded mysterious earlier," she said as she sat down. "What's going on?"

I laughed quietly.

"Nothing bad," I reassured her. "But there's something I wanted to tell you both."

A few moments later Stephanie appeared as well, full of her usual energy, greeting us both with a cheerful wave as she joined the table.

Once the waiter had taken our drinks order and the first drinks had arrived, I explained the situation.

"I've been asked to return to the UK," I said, keeping my voice calm but unable to hide the slight excitement behind the words.

"In a few weeks."

Both of them looked surprised at first.

"You're leaving Mallorca?" Stephanie asked.

"For a while," I replied. "It's another role with the company. I'll be covering maternity leave back in the UK for a few months. After that… who knows where they want me."

Alison leaned back slightly in her chair, taking a moment to absorb the news.

"Well," she said eventually with a small smile, "that sounds like a good thing."

"It is," I admitted. "It's part of the career path, really, what I signed up for when I joined the company."

The conversation that followed carried a mixture of emotions. There was genuine happiness about the opportunity ahead, but also the quiet understanding that my time on the island was drawing to a close.

We talked about the season so far, about some of the ridiculous situations we had faced and the small moments that had made us laugh at the time. The long airport delays, the strange guest requests, the unexpected problems that had somehow become stories worth remembering.

It felt less like a farewell and more like a quiet recognition that we had all shared something unique.

Working abroad creates a particular kind of friendship. When people live and work together far from home, sharing both the pressures and the adventures of the job, the bonds form quickly and often deeply.

Those evenings together, the laughter, the conversations and the shared memories of the season, were part of what made the experience so special.

At one point Alison raised her glass slightly.

"To Mallorca," she said with a smile.

Stephanie laughed.

"And to wherever Wesley ends up next, lucky sod."

I lifted my own glass.

"To the adventure," I said.

And for a moment, the three of us simply sat there, enjoying the warm evening air and the quiet knowledge that whatever happened next, the time we had shared on that island would always remain part of our story.

Alison leaned slightly closer across the table and lowered her voice with a small smile.

"I'm going to miss you more than most," she said.

I laughed and waved the comment away lightly.

"Well," I replied, "you just like having a toy boy around."

"You cheeky whatsit!" she fired back, laughing as she nudged my arm.

But beneath the humour, I understood exactly what she meant.

We had never really described what existed between us. We weren't officially dating, and neither of us had ever tried to define the relationship in those terms. Yet over the course of the time in Mallorca, we had grown very close.

There had been evenings spent together talking long after our shifts had ended, and more than once she had stayed the night in my room.

In fact, it happened often enough that I occasionally joked about it.

"Why do you even bother?" I once said to her with a smile. "You live next door."

She had simply laughed.

But those small, unspoken moments were part of what made the experience abroad feel so real. When you live and work in the same place, sharing long days, late nights and the occasional madness that comes with the job, connections form naturally.

Some of them were friendships.

Others, like the one Alison and I shared, sat somewhere quietly in between.

And now, as we sat together that evening, knowing my time on the island was drawing to a close, there was an unspoken understanding that those moments, too, would soon become memories.

Later that evening, after dinner had come to a gentle close, I found myself walking slowly along the bay of Palma Nova.

The night air was warm and calm, the kind of soft Mediterranean evening that seems to settle quietly over the coastline once the last light of the day fades from the sky.

Along the water's edge, the lights from the hotels and restaurants reflected gently across the bay, small twinkling patterns dancing across the surface of the sea as the tide moved slowly against the shore.

It was one of those peaceful moments when the resort seemed to pause for a while.

The music from nearby bars drifted softly through the air, mixed with the distant murmur of conversations and the occasional laughter of guests enjoying the warm evening. Somewhere further along the promenade, a guitarist was playing quietly outside a café, adding a relaxed rhythm to the night.

I walked slowly, taking it all in.

My face still felt pleasantly warm from the day's sunshine, and I couldn't help but smile slightly at the thought that, despite being a redhead, the island had somehow managed to give me a rather respectable golden tan, and my hair was golden now in colour, a real strawberry blonde. Not bad at all for someone whose skin had once spent most of its time beneath grey English skies.

Looking out across the bay, it struck me how familiar the place had become.

Only a few months earlier, I had arrived on the island feeling slightly unsure of what lay ahead. Now the promenade, the beach and the lights reflecting across the water all felt like part of my daily life.

Places that once seemed foreign had quietly become familiar.

And perhaps that is one of the most beautiful things about living abroad, even if only for a short time. What begins as an unknown place slowly becomes somewhere you understand, somewhere you belong, if only temporarily.

Standing there for a moment, watching the gentle movement of the sea beneath the lights of Palma Nova, I realised that the island had left its mark on me in ways I was only beginning to understand.

Mallorca had given me more than a job.

It had given me a chapter of life that I knew I would never forget.

I had not been standing there for very long when I heard footsteps approaching behind me along the promenade.

I turned slightly and saw Alison walking toward me.

She had clearly taken the same idea as I had, stepping out into the warm evening air for a quiet walk after dinner. The soft lights from the nearby cafés caught her face as she drew closer, and she smiled when she saw me standing by the rail looking out across the water.

"I thought I might find you out here," she said.

I laughed softly.

"It seemed like the right place to be tonight."

She came to stand beside me, and for a moment neither of us said very much. We simply looked out across the bay together, watching the lights of Palma Nova shimmer gently across the dark water.

The evening had that calm, settled feeling that sometimes arrives late in the Mediterranean night, when the day's energy begins to fade, and the island seems to breathe a little more slowly.

"You'll miss this place," she said eventually.

I nodded.

"Yes… I think I will."

It was a simple admission, but it carried more meaning than the words alone suggested. Mallorca had quietly woven itself into my life during those months, and the thought of leaving it behind now felt strangely significant.

Alison leaned slightly on the rail beside me.

"You've done well here, you know," she said. "Not everyone settles in so quickly, and you're so young."

I smiled, remembering the early days when I had felt anything but confident.

"I think the island helped," I replied. "It has a way of teaching you things."

She glanced at me with a knowing expression.

"That it does."

For a while, we continued walking slowly along the promenade, the gentle sound of the sea accompanying our steps. Couples strolled past in the opposite direction, and somewhere behind us, the soft music from a nearby bar drifted across the warm evening air.

Eventually, we paused again near the edge of the bay.

"You're going to do well, wherever they send you next," Alison said quietly.

I looked out across the water once more.

"Maybe," I replied. "But I'll always remember where it started."

She smiled at that, and for a moment the two of us stood there together in comfortable silence, watching the lights of Palma Nova reflecting across the Mediterranean.

Some places stay with you long after you leave them.

Mallorca, I knew even then, would be one of those places.

After a while, I turned to Alison and said something that had been quietly sitting in the back of my mind.

"Shall we stay in touch?" I asked.

She looked at me for a moment before smiling gently and shaking her head.

"No," she said softly. "I don't think that's a good idea. Not in this job."

I raised an eyebrow slightly, surprised by the answer. She looked out across the bay again before continuing.

"But if our paths cross one day again, and they might," she said, "then that would be nice."

There was no sadness in her voice when she said it. In fact, there was something quite wise about the way she looked at it.

"Let's just leave it as it is," she said with a small smile. "A lovely friendship, Wesley."

I nodded.

"Yes," I replied. "You're right."

And that was that.

There are moments in life that don't need promises or plans for the future. Sometimes it is enough simply to recognise that a particular time and place have been special and to allow it to remain exactly that.

The truth is, I did see Alison again, many years later.

I was passing through London Heathrow Airport when I suddenly spotted a familiar face moving quickly through the terminal in a British Airways uniform. For a moment, I wasn't quite sure, but as she drew closer, I realised it was her.

"Alison!" I called out.

She turned, recognised me instantly, and ran over with a huge smile before wrapping me in a warm hug.

"Wesley!" she laughed. "I can't believe it's you."

We spoke only briefly. Airports have a way of keeping people moving, and she was clearly rushing between flights. But she looked genuinely pleased to see me, and for a few minutes it felt as though the years between Mallorca and that airport terminal had quietly disappeared.

Then she hurried off again, disappearing back into the flow of travellers and airline crew.

And that was the last time I ever saw her. Perhaps our paths will cross again somewhere, someday. I like to think that they might. After all travel has made the world a small place.

Over the following days the rhythm of life in Mallorca continued much as it always had.

Guests arrived, others departed, excursions ran as usual and the steady hum of resort life carried on along the familiar promenade of Palma Nova. Yet for me there was now a quiet awareness that my own time on the island was drawing gently to a close.

There were small moments during those final days when I caught myself pausing more than usual. Walking along the beach early in the morning before the resort fully woke, standing for a moment on the promenade watching the fishing boats out in the bay, or simply sitting with a coffee in one of the cafés that had become so familiar.

Places that had once felt new now felt almost like home.

Eventually the morning of my departure arrived.

It was one of those bright Mediterranean mornings where the sky seemed impossibly blue and the air already carried the warmth of the day ahead. I packed my suitcase slowly, folding the last few shirts and placing them carefully inside, aware that this simple act marked the end of an important chapter of my life.

Outside, the resort was already beginning to stir. Guests were drifting toward breakfast, the sound of plates and cutlery carrying faintly through the hotel restaurant while cleaners moved quietly along the corridors beginning another day.

I took one last look from the balcony toward the sea.

The Mediterranean lay calm and wide beneath the morning sun, the same view that had greeted me so many times during my stay. For a moment I simply stood there, committing the scene quietly to memory.

Then it was time to leave.

The transfer coach arrived along the promenade shortly afterwards, the driver greeting me with the relaxed nod that seemed universal among Spanish drivers. My suitcase was placed gently in the luggage hold and I climbed aboard, taking a seat near the front as we pulled slowly away from Palma Nova.

The journey to Palma Airport did not take long.

The road followed the curve of the coastline for a while before venturing through Palma toward the airport itself. Along the way I watched the island pass quietly through the window, the beaches, the cafés, the palm trees lining the roads.

All the small details that had become part of daily life.

It struck me then how strange travel can be.

A place that once felt completely foreign can slowly become familiar, almost comfortable, and then suddenly you find yourself leaving it behind.

Before long the airport buildings appeared ahead of us.

Palma Airport had already become a familiar place during my time on the island, yet that morning it felt slightly different knowing I was now travelling as a passenger rather than working as a rep.

Check-in was quick and uneventful.

Soon I found myself seated by the window of the aircraft as it taxied slowly toward the runway. Outside, the warm Mallorcan sunshine reflected brightly off the wings while the distant outline of the Tramuntana mountains could still just be seen on the horizon.

The engines began to build power.

Moments later, the aircraft lifted smoothly into the Mediterranean sky, the island slowly shrinking beneath us as the coastline faded gently into the distance.

A few hours later, we descended through a very different sky.

The clouds were thick and grey as the aircraft approached London Gatwick, the familiar dull light of an English afternoon waiting below us. As we touched down on the runway and the wheels met the tarmac, I couldn't help but smile slightly to myself.

The weather might have been grey and the air considerably cooler, but I knew something important.

This wasn't the end of the journey.

In many ways, it was only just beginning.

Mallorca had been my first real chapter of life abroad.

And I had a strong feeling that many more adventures were still waiting somewhere beyond the horizon.

As I stepped through the arrivals doors at Gatwick, pulling my suitcase behind me, the familiar hum of the terminal surrounded me once again. Families were greeting loved ones, drivers held up signs for arriving passengers, and the unmistakable smell of coffee drifted through the hall. And then, across the small crowd waiting behind the barrier, I saw a face I knew better than any other.

My father.

He stood there quietly, hands resting on the rail, watching the passengers emerge one by one. When he saw me, he smiled, that steady, reassuring smile that only a father can give, and raised his hand in a small wave.

In that moment, I realised something simple but powerful. The world might be vast and full of distant places, but the journeys that shape us most often begin and end with the people who believed in us before we ever set out.

I walked over and gave him a hug, feeling once again the familiar comfort of home after months away.

"Well," he said with a grin, "how was Majorca then?"

I smiled.

"Just the beginning, just the beginning", I replied.

And as we walked out of the airport together into the cool English air, I knew with quiet certainty that somewhere out there, beyond the grey skies and familiar roads of home, the next adventure was already waiting…

Acknowledgements

I would like to dedicate this book to the memory of my late father, who passed away on 24 January 2024. His belief in me never wavered, even during the times when I was still trying to discover who I was and where life might take me. His quiet strength and steady encouragement remain a guiding light in everything I do.

To my wife, who has walked beside me through the many chapters of life, including some difficult health battles in recent years. Your calm strength, loyalty and unwavering support have meant more than words can ever truly express.

To my daughter, Arabella, and my son, Thomas, you are my greatest adventure. Your love, laughter and belief in me continue to inspire everything I do.

To the many people I met during my time overseas in those early years, fellow representatives, hotel teams, drivers, guides, bar staff, receptionists, chefs, waiters and the wonderful housekeeping staff who quietly kept everything running behind the scenes, thank you. Your kindness, humour and generosity turned workplaces into communities and strangers into friends.

To the people of Mallorca, whose beautiful island offered far more than sunshine and beaches. It gave me lessons, friendships, culture and experiences that helped shape the person I was becoming. For that, I will always remain grateful, and I have returned many times as a traveller, but maybe one day, who knows, I may return to live again.

To the fellow reps who shared the long days, the unexpected challenges and the late-night laughter that only those who have lived the overseas life, truly understand, thank you for the camaraderie and the memories.

To Alison, whose friendship brought warmth, laughter and a touch of magic to those days on the island. Wherever life has taken you now, I hope the world has treated you kindly.

And to those quiet moments that travel sometimes gifts us, the unexpected conversations, the small cafés, the mountain roads and the people we meet along the way, thank you for reminding me that the world is always far richer than we imagine.

To Sue and Andrew Wittich for being just an incredible couple of friends and for providing encouragement to continue to write.

To Chris Conway for being a lifelong friend and for taking it upon himself to stock and sell my books in his incredible shop in Whitstable.

Finally, to you, the reader.

Thank you for travelling with me once again. I hope these pages allowed you to step into another time and another place, to feel the sunshine, the excitement of youth and the quiet wonder of discovering the world for the first time.

Finally, take a moment to listen to your body, to the birds and insects outside your home, wherever that may be, and slow down, as life is precious. Live for today, always. The world is a beautiful place and let travel open your eyes to all its wonders.

Where the Journey Continues…

As the final pages of this story close, the sun is still setting somewhere over the waters of the Mediterranean, casting its golden glow across the beautiful island of Mallorca.

From the lively promenades of Palma Nova and the historic streets of Palma to the quiet mountain villages of the Tramuntana and the hidden coves scattered along the island's rugged coastline, Mallorca is far more than a holiday destination. It is an island of stories, culture, laughter, friendships and moments that stay with you long after the journey ends.

Explore Mallorca

Discover more about this extraordinary island through the official travel guide: www.visitmallorca.com

Travel Inspiration

For travel articles, stories and ideas to spark your next adventure, visit: www.purevacations.com

Book Your Experience

PURE ONE Travel offers unforgettable journeys across Europe and beyond, created by travellers who believe that the best adventures are the ones that stay with you forever. www.pureonetravel.com

Because some journeys begin the moment you turn the final page.

"Els camins que recorrem es converteixen en
records que mai abandonen el cor."

The roads we travel become memories that never leave the
heart.

Other Books…

Book Titles by Wesley Baker:

Echoes Travel Memoirs:
Echoes of a Season
Spanish Sunshine
Echoes in Andalusia
Echoes in Mallorca

Novels:
The Spy Who Found Me

Signed Copies Available:
www.wesleybaker.com

More stories will follow,
Keep an eye on the horizon.